Pro Se Prisoner:

C.A. Knuckles

Freebird Publishers
North Dighton, MA

Freebird Publishers

221 Pearl St., Ste. 541, North Dighton, MA 02764
Info@FreebirdPublishers.com
FreebirdPublishers.com

All Freebird Publishers titles, imprints, and distributed lines are available at special quantity discounts for bulk purchases for sales promotions, premiums, fundraising educational or institutional use.

ISBN: 978-1-952159-24-4

Printed in the United States of America

Warning-Disclaimer: This book is informational and doesn't constitute financial advice. Please don't assume that all financial information will apply to you. This is not a get-rich-quick scheme. Consult a financial adviser before applying the information in this book to your own portfolio or before making any investments detailed in this book.

I will always dedicate everything I do to those I lost too soon: my mother, grandmother, grandfather, K. "Fat Cat" Lewis, and N. "Devon" Sassafras – may you rest in peace. I will hold on to the memories we created together.

Acknowledgements

I would like to acknowledge Freebird Publishers for giving a voice to the voiceless. They are dedicated to the incarcerated prisoners around this country and dedicated to the advancement of our knowledge – one book at a time. Thank you for your help; without all of you, none of this would have been possible.

Knowledge Seekers

There are two types…

"Hedgehogs" gravitate to a specific field and burrow deep, eventually becoming the talking we see on TV.

"'Foxes,'" on the other hand, cast a wider net, constantly seeking out new information to challenge what they know. Super forecasters are overwhelmingly the latter…their defining characteristic is 'an openness to treat their beliefs as testable hypotheses and not sacred possessions.'"

– Philip Tetlock, as quoted in the Wall Street Journal (with apologies to Isaiah Berlin)

Which one are you?

Contents

Introduction

Look around the prison and you will see all types of people –
some lost, others conducting business, others reading the
newspaper. As I sit in prison, I see opportunity, with the added
bonus of time to prepare, study, and take action.

Most grew up in poverty, abject poverty, without any financial
knowledge beyond selling drugs on the corner – where 99% fail,
get killed, or end up in prison before age 21. To be honest I was
lost at first, never dumb, just lost. I was following instead of
leading, looking at people who never cared or had my best
interest in mind. So, one day I asked myself, "What's your
endgame? What is your plan? What are you passionate about?
Who are you?"

Those questions led me to my passion: helping and creating
opportunities for prisoners and poor people. I studied the rich,
the "One Percent," so I could use their skills and financial
knowledge to help myself and others get ahead. The rich know
that to create long-term wealth you must first have financial
literacy, the ability to understand and effectively use various
financial skills, including personal financial
management, budgeting, and investing. The second thing you
must have been an actionable plan – a sequence of steps that
must be taken, or activities that must be performed well, for a
strategy to succeed. And third, you need to learn the tax code.

My goal is to help you obtain wealth from prison by showing you
what the rich do and how to legally play within their system to
beat them at their own game. You have the pleasure of time on
your side to study, create a plan, act on that plan, and create
wealth from right where you are. I call this "self-help business," a
mental plan for financial success. It's time to free your mind.

"Give a man a fish and you feed him for a day; teach a man to
fish and you feed him for a lifetime." Showing you how to
succeed and giving you the knowledge of financial literacy will

help you along the way, but it's up to you to act on that knowledge to create opportunity for others and wealth for yourself. This book is your start.

Part One:
Financial Knowledge

Getting Your Mind Right

Money is a complex subject that's not taught in the inner cities of our country. Our only experience with it is in the streets hustling and selling drugs.

Ninety-five percent of the drug dealers out there selling products are never successful. It really turns into the same thing as a person working, living paycheck-to-paycheck. One bad thing happens – an unexpected medical expense, car accident, or arrest – and you are back at square one, broke with the rent due and the car payments behind.

It's just more complex for the dealers because bad financial decisions are already part of the game. Most would rather buy an ounce of crack and use the revenue to get fresh, buy clothes, shoes, and a car, with no way of re-upping. Instead of buying more product with the proceeds, they squander the money because they lack financial literacy. Ask a drug dealer to show you his "Profit and Loss" statements.

While the government sits back and watches, they allow you to make your money and then use arcane drug laws to put you in prison for long periods of time. They take your money, prosecute you with it, and then put you in prison and profit from your incarceration. It's a win-win for them, and we just keep feeding the system.

Our lack of financial knowledge is deeply linked to our environment. Now is your turn to gain that knowledge and execute a sound financial management plan and stock strategy. I have put together some general info that should help you out along your way.

Becoming financially independent is the goal. This will open more doors to become an "owner." You can't create long-term wealth without being an owner: working for someone else will not work. Being an employee is not the way. You must start your own business and make a difference. But before you start, ask yourself some simple questions:

1. What's your passion?

2. If you could do anything with your time, what would it be?

3. How would you achieve your passion?

More than Money

Now look at how you view money. You must master it, but you must master yourself first. Prepare your mind and you can begin to find your passion and form a plan to execute it.

The reason why drug dealers fail is because money can't change who you are – it just magnifies your lack of financial literacy. We believe that money changes us, but money without financial knowledge will always end in failure. Gain the knowledge, create a plan, and execute that plan.

Take investing for example: to be successful all you have to do is grow your savings to a point where your investments will generate enough income for you to live on and invest further, as you wish. So, the best way to invest now is for the long-term. This can be accomplished through low-cost index funds and dividend-producing companies. We will get into these specifics as we go.

Who to Study

The "One Percent" doesn't lose playing the market because they make the rules. But you can study their moves and learn from them. Buying low-cost indexes is good for a portion of your investment money, but even with them you must spread it out a little bit. Everything has risks, but stocks are still your best investment for long term growth. That's why to lower the risk you must diversify your investments across multiple indexes.

An index is a list of stocks, like the S&P 500. This market will show an aggregate of all 500 stocks in that index. Instead of buying or trying to beat the market, you diversify and get a percentage of all 500 stocks in the index. Besides the S&P, there is a real estate index, a short-term bond index, a gold index, and a commodities index. Remember to invest in the market, not the individual stock. In my next stock book, I will show you these methods. In this book we will be covering the nuts and bolts and building you a base to start with. Dividend-producing stocks will be your foundation.

Asset Allocation

The biggest and most successful investment strategy I learned from the One Percent is "Asset Allocation." You must understand that along the way you will learn multiple tips and tricks from stock books and so-called professionals, but we are trying to get wealthy and stay wealthy. The One Percent do this is with Asset Allocation.

What is it? Asset Allocation is basically dividing your money among different classes of investments, which allows you to balance your risk and return. You place percentages of money in different areas, such as stocks, bonds, real estate, and bitcoins.

You fine-tune this balance to decrease your risk and increase your returns, and it's free!

Rule 1: Don't Lose Money
Rule 2: See Rule 1.
– Warren Buffet

Pick classes and income you are willing to invest and diversify across multiple classes. The next step in Asset Allocation is dollar-cost averaging. We know how to diversify across asset classes and across markets. When you invest in a set time and pattern each week or month, with the same amount of money that's in line with your asset allocation plan, the fluctuations of the market work to increase your gains. This allows you to make higher gains regularly in a volatile stock market. Buying more when the index is cheaper allows you to own more of the market when prices rise.

Constantly check yourself and your plan on a weekly basis. Analyze your losses, examine your successes, and learn by execution, not sitting on the sidelines "wishing." In prison you have nothing but time to become a great investor.

Compounding Savings

Another way to get your financial IQ up is to put it to work compounding savings. Set aside a portion of your money orders each time you get one. If you work in prison, set aside a portion of that also. This will be the starting point of your money plan; this will allow you to invest with confidence and intelligence. The goal is to stop working for money—and let money work for you.

Nine-to-five jobs are what rich people hope you will do after college and prison – work for them and take your paycheck to pay down college debt and service fees for parole and probation. The system wants you to be like a hamster on the wheel, go into more debt or violate and come back to prison, instead of controlling your own finances and building your own business. Being in prison is even worse, because you work for pennies per hour and then give it right back to the "contract industry" of prison (commissary, sick-call co-pays, catalog orders, etc.)

Financial literacy is the best way to capitalize on this path forward to financial freedom. You have time to sit in a cell and study stock charts and become a successful investor. When people are afraid to invest, you climb in and buy; these are the best chances to gain an edge in the markets.

By using compounding savings to invest wisely each month, you will gain huge interest on your money. Set aside a percentage of your income every month and stick to it. Use this money for your investment. Once your investments begin to pay off and your income increases, you can set aside a larger percentage for investing. As you continue to gain from your savings, eventually you will be able to live entirely off the interest!

It doesn't take much to live in prison. But remember your biggest goal is saving for when you are released. By investing and saving on a per month basis for the remainder of your incarceration, while also reinvesting the income and dividends for compound growth, you will be able to accumulate massive savings. This will enable you to start a business, buy a house, and land on your feet upon release.

Invest the difference across the market in low S&P 500 Index funds. This index is a cross section of the whole market. As prisoners, we are not trying to beat the market, but invest for the long-term. That's what compound saving, and Asset Allocation are about. Financial Knowledge is the key: so, keep learning, studying, and mentally growing.

Reaching your goals in prison is about your frame of mind; change that and you're set to change your circumstances. – C. A. Knuckles

What Blocks Success

As a prisoner we tend to make excuses about why we can't do something. But over the years what I have seen is that it's easier for us to make excuses than it is for us to obtain the knowledge to succeed in life. So, what is it that you as a prisoner want out of life?

Freedom is good, as most would answer, but are you mentally ready for freedom? That entails not coming back to prison, setting up a financial plan, and pursuing that plan with actions and determination.

Money is always a goal upon release but wanting money and having the plan together to keep the money is a whole other story. It's been said that "a man that fails to plan, plans to fail." So, the question is, "How do you plan to obtain the finances necessary to maintain your freedom"? Without an answer to that question, you are just wishing for freedom and financial success.

We as prisoners must set up our mind to believe that we accomplish anything right now while incarcerated. Our main thing is our negative mindset that blocks us from success. Once we take ownership of our mindset and stop passing blame to others, we will conquer our dreams.

In most cases abject poverty and living in improvised ghettos ultimately led us to prison. And prison was the result of the problem. The start of the problem was not having the knowledge and education to get out of poverty.

We all said that we were selling drugs to help our family, but once we make some money, we forget about the family. Then we adopt the go-to phrase, "I'm hustling to get out the hood." But the hustling never stops when the money is made. The result is always the same: we get busted. Welcome to the hamster wheel.

Because his daily thoughts were centered on prison, he received prison. – A prison author

Fill in the blank: I am _____.
Think before you fill in the blank, because what you think of yourself will be in full view for you to see. Now ask another person, someone who knows you well, to fill in the same blank for you on another piece of paper. I am _____. Now compare the two and see if you (inside) see the same as other people (outside) see.

With both answers down, you are probably somewhere in the middle. How you view yourself is usually about fifty percent right and how others see you is usually about fifty percent correct – you fall in the middle. The only thing that will change either of these perspectives is how you think. As you think, so you are!

We must be mentally sound and have the financial knowledge to succeed before we start buying stocks, start a company, or invest in anything. Even more importantly, we can't mentally block ourselves from success. We must be able to think past the 4 corners of our cells. We must not lock our mind into isolation, like our physical bodies are. Financial success starts with mental success – releasing and unlearning bad blockers that hinder us from thinking about becoming wealthy.

Financial Thoughts

To close this out, a few more thought to get you the financial knowledge and mental knowledge to succeed at every corner. Prison is a paradox: In the midst of cruel punishment there is also self-rehabilitation by prisoners determined to change. Judges don't sentence you to get rehabilitated, it's strictly for punishment. It's up to us as prisoners to change our mindset and be that success story.

Being confined to a cell or in prison itself, will cause you to tap into the deepest parts of the mind and self
– C. A. Knuckles

We as prisoners should be in search of and chasing total financial self-reliance and not working a part-time job once released. Learn to write a business and financial plan (my next financial book will show you how), not just resumes. Creating jobs is better than applying for jobs. Not having that financial knowledge narrows your vision to see the trap you're in without it. Intelligence solves problems and produces money every single time.

Instead of growing up wanting to be a famous athlete, movie star, rapper, or the biggest drug dealer, learn to be the owner and CEO of your own empire of companies. People who struggle are often the result of people working for someone else.

You came to prison with nothing, don't leave with nothing – gain financial knowledge. Stocks and Bitcoins are the start, my next book will get into starting a business from prison, Venture Capital investments, funding, taxes, and multiple forms of alternative investments. Now let's get started building you a strong financial foundation.

Part Two:
Buying Stock

Impossible is just a big word thrown around by small men who find it easier to live in the world they've been given than to explore the power they have to change it. Impossible is not a fact. It's an option. Impossible is not a declaration, it's a dare. Impossible is potential. Impossible is temporary. Impossible is nothing.
– Unknown

Will you use your power to explore?

Chapter 1

A Brief Overview
of the Stock Market

Lock my body, can't trap my mind.
– Jay-Z (Reasonable Doubt)

To really get history correct about this prominent, established institution, we must travel back to a time in our history when our country didn't treat every human being as equal. During slavery Wall Street was not the same as we know it today. In its early history, the stock market was a place where slaves were being brought and sold on the daily basis, as if they were common commodities. This in turn made New York City one of the best major cities in the world.

As we have seen through history, the past has a crazy way of popping back up in the future, and it always humbles you. The fact that now a descendant of these same slaves that were sold against their will has a chance to buy and sell stocks from that same spot, is a humbling experience. Also, to be able to educate the lowest rung of the new caste system – prison slaves – on how to buy stocks to make them financially free from the prison industrial complex is a real warm and fulfilling thing.

Stocks can be purchased in many different ways; they are shares in a publicly traded company. Stocks are risky, but as with everything else in life education and gaining knowledge is the key. On the open market you can purchase many different securities. Some are:

CDs – Certificates of Deposit; they are a time deposit – a financial product commonly sold by banks, thrift institutions, and credit unions. CDs differ from savings accounts in that the **CD** has a specific, fixed term (often one, three, or six months, or one to ten years) and usually, a fixed interest rate. The interest rates are low, but this is a real low-risk investment.

Bonds – U.S. government saving bonds, issued at face value. Savings bonds are debt securities issued by the U.S. Department of the Treasury to help pay for the U.S. government's borrowing needs. U.S. savings bonds are considered one of the safest investments because they are backed by the full faith and credit of the U.S. government. These are long-term investments and are seen as alternatives to CDs. The most important thing to know is that you can be assessed a penalty for selling them before maturity.

Real Estate (REIT) – Real Estate Investment Trust gives you the chance to make low-cost investments in large-scale, income-producing properties. By law they must payout 90% of profits in dividends.

Mutual Funds – These are managed by professionals; People pay big firms to invest in a pool of stocks or securities on their behalf. Always do research on these and make sure your strategies are the same.

In this part, I will focus on regular stocks on the open market for publicly traded companies, but from time-to-time one or two of the above securities will be in reference in relation to publicly traded stocks.

Stocks are sold in two different markets. The first is the "primary market," and second is a "stock exchange," which is also the secondary market. The top 7 major stock exchanges are:

- New York Stock Exchange (NXSE)

- Nasdaq (NASDAQ)

- Japan Exchange Group (JPX)

- London Stock Exchange (LSE)

- Shanghai Stock Exchange (SSE)

- Hong Kong Stock Exchange (SEHK)

- Euronext

Historically people have always been left out of the market for reasons that have to do with finances. Poor people under the poverty line think that the market is fixed, and they can't invest. I used to have these same thoughts, until I started to do my own research on this topic. Being in prison opened my eyes to the stock market. Stock investing can be done right from your prison cell, now! This book will teach you how.

Prison has conditioned us not to seek information and fall down the repeated cycle of this crooked system. I choose to not fall for that misguided thought process. If you're reading this book, then you feel the same way as many others.

DRIPs (Dividend Reinvestment Program) allow you to take control of your future finances now. With as little as $25 dollars you will gain financial freedom from your cell. I will also show you how to invest on the open markets through online discount brokers, where you can set up an account from your support system on the streets.

But you cannot rely on others for answers. To control your investments and make money, you *must* get companies' annual and quarterly reports and read them. You can obtain the quarterly earnings report of each and every company you wish to invest in before investing at sec.gov. You may also obtain the report by writing to the SEC directly and asking for a copy. The address is provided in the "Resources to Help" section of the book.

Newspapers are also a must. You will have to read the newspapers to stay in tune with all the news affecting the stocks you have invested in. So, the focus is on the now. This is not a get-rich-quick scheme, but a thinking, hard work thing. Your investment will only pay off with hard work and dedication.

So, you might be asking yourself, "What are stocks?" Stocks are shares of public-traded companies. They allow citizens to become part owners of corporations. This would include the likes of Amazon, Facebook, Twitter, and even Elon Musk's Telsa. Once you have purchased stock you will be given a stock certificate, which is an investment evidencing ownership of one or more shares of the corporation.

The stock exchange is the place where security trading is conducted in an organized system. You, as the person buying the stock, become an owner of corporation stock.

You will also need to know what indexes you will be buying the stocks from. The Stock Market is broken down into multiple indexes that have their own purposes and stocks. First, let's start with these:

- **Standard & Poor's 500 (S&P500)** – This index is a broader, more modern representation of market action than the Dow. Consist of 500 companies.

- **The NASDAQ Composite (NASDAQ)** – This index is somewhat more volatile and relevant index in recent years. The NASDAQ is home to many of the market's younger, more innovative, and fast-growing companies that trade via the Nasdaq network of market makers. It's a little more weighted toward the technology sector.

- **The Dow Jones Industrial Average (D.J.I.A.)** – Consist of 30 widely-traded big-cap stocks. It is a rather out-of-date average to study because it consists of large, established, old line companies rather than today's more entrepreneurial concerns.

- **The NYSE Composite (NYSE)** – This is an index of all stocks listed on the New York Stock Exchange.

Just so we are clear, financial freedom doesn't come easy in this regard, but nothing in life comes easy. Building your financial IQ is the only way to level the playing field. So here is a little bit more educational information.

The quarterly corporate earnings statement comes out every three months, meaning there are four each year. You will need to read these carefully after studying the company's annual earnings (AE) growth rate. Look at the AE to see the increase of each of the past 3 years. You don't want to see the second year's earnings down, out of 3 years, even if the 3rd year has higher earnings. Strong earnings in the last several quarters, plus solid growth in recent years, is what to look for.

Over the years you probably have heard people refer to the P/E ratios. This is the price-earnings ratio, which relates a company's share price to its earnings per share. A high P/E ratio could mean that a company's stock is over-valued, or else that investors are expecting high growth rates in the future. So, the important thing to look for is stock that is undervalued (if the P/E is low), which means it should be bought. If it is overvalued (the P/E is high), then it should be sold.

Just so you are well informed, the stock market sometimes plays around with this number, so it's not always relevant in price movement, and has little to do with if some stocks should be brought. You must leverage this information against other tools and the overall sum of the information you have gathered in making buying decisions. The P/E is not a standalone factor to determine whether to invest in a particular stock or not.

Stocks come in two forms "common" and "preferred." The main thing to remember is the dividend; that is the biggest difference between the two. Being a preferred shareholder puts that stockholder in a more exclusive position than the holder of common stock. When liquidation happens, the dividend is a reward or profit the company gives a stockholder for investing in a company. This is done monthly, quarterly, or yearly depending on the company's policy. Preferred stockholders always get dividends paid in full before common stockholders.

This is not a get-rich-quick scheme, understanding the history of the stock market and raising your financial IQ is the only way to gain capital from the stock market. The four (4) laws of financial IQ are:

1. Accounting – ability to read numbers

2. Investing – investing is the science of money-making money

3. Markets – understanding markets is the science of supply and demand

4. Law – understanding the tax advantages

– Source: Tony Robbins, *Money Master the Game* (2014)

Chapter 2

A Brief Overview of the Stock Market

Reaching your goals in prison is about your frame of mind; change that and you're set to change your circumstances. – C. A. Knuckles

Since this how-to book is for the prisoner who wants to stop giving their money to commissary, prison catalogs, etc., I'm going to present this information in a straightforward way as if you know nothing about the stock market and investing.

As with Bitcoins, so with stocks first comes the research, then the knowledge, then the picks. Upfront, let's get a few things out the way first. One of the most important things that you would need to know is how to read stock and newspaper stock charts.

%CHG	52-week Hi	52-week Lo	STOCK	SYM	YLD %	PE	LAST	NET CHG
-13.76	28.67	21.92	ABB	ABB	3.6	24	23.14	0.03
4.56	46.19	37.66	Aflac	AFL	2.3	8	45.89	0.21
-12.99	39.80	31.17	AT&T	T	5.9	7	33.83	0.02
3.85	125.86	68.72	Abbvie	ABBV	3.8	25	100.43	1.11
-10.51	105.36	85.59	Allstate	ALL	2.0	10	93.71	0.51
44.00	1714.50	927.00	Amazon.com	AMZN	000	212	1683.99	-5.31
-4.92	81.98	68.28	Cincinnati.Com	CINF	3.0	15	71.28	0.51
-4.21	48.62	36.17	Coca-Cola	KO	3.5	137	43.95	0.51
-3.12	13.48	10.14	Fordmotor	F	2.3	27	58.92	1.27
-4.91	20.25	11.12	FreeportMCM	FCX	.....	12	18.03	0.10
-16.18	56.95	39.34	Harley Davidson	HOG	3.5	14	42.65	0.10
30.22	65.89	37.25	Hess	HES	1.6	dd	61.84	-0.49
4.64	207.60	144.25	HomeDepot	HD	2.1	26	198.33	2.16
28.53	166.64	98.27	IAC/Inter Active	IAC	.....	44	157.17	1.04
1.54	111.46	90.25	McCormick	MKC	2.0	17	103.34	2.43
19.74	75.91	50.35	Nike	NKE	1.1	71	74.90	0.14
16.28	58.37	41.03	NovoNordisk	NVO	1.8	18	44.93	-1.08
35.55	266.59	138.58	NVIDIA	NVDA	0.2	44	262.28	-0.62
78.19	62.83	22.41	Square	SQ	.....	dd	61.78	1.11
2.03	389.61	244.59	Tesla	TLSA	.....	dd	317.66	1.57
10.82	120.75	75.92	Texas Instruments	TXN	2.1	29	115.74	-1.50
-12.23	259.77	191.44	3M	MMM	2.6	31	206.59	1.52
27.17	132.21	86.15	Tiffany	TIF	1.7	39	132.19	0.20
4.23	103.90	85.88	TimeWarner	TWX	1.7	14	95.34	-0.03

As the stock chart from the *Wall Street Journal* shows, there are important features that stand out. The first is the stock column where you will find the company's name. In the symbol (SYM) column you will find the "ticker" symbol (*ex.* AbbVie's symbol is "ABBV"). This is the company's personal symbol. No two companies have the same symbol, like no two people have the same fingerprint. Close to that, you'll find the "PE," which is the "price per earnings" ratio – we touched on that a couple of pages ago. Next would be the "EPS," which is a rating scale of 1 to 99, with 99 being the best. An EPS of 99 means that a company has outperformed 99% of all other companies in terms of both annual and recent quarterly earnings performance.

Remember, when looking at the charts keep in mind that all companies are not listed on the same exchange, as the above list may show. Newspapers and websites just put them in alphabetical order.

Always consult with a professional
before using these methods.

You will also see these: "DIV," "CHG," and "52-week high." The "DIV" is short for dividend and is the dollar amounts the company pays out in dividends. The "CHG" is the last close percentage from the previous trading day's closes. And the "52-week high" shows trading range for the past year. One more would be the "Yield," which is the return to shareholders. This depends on the stock price and current dividend. That's your crash course in stock chart reading.

There is much more financial jargon out there, but we have covered the most important of them in the last two chapters. There are many ways that you can purchase stocks from prison. If you have a support system out there in the free world that will be a good resource. Others, like me, don't have those computer savvy people to assist them, so you must do things on your own. It takes time to do, so don't give up.

As a first-time stock buyer, even if you understand stocks and the market, you might not know how to play the market wisely. First you need to gather all the free information you can before investing. That can be found by getting outside people in your network to go to: yahoofinance.com or download the app. This app allows you to sync portfolios and quotes across multiple devices – tracking stock, currencies, commodities and more. Yahoo allows you to check on any company's stock price and get information about the stock you need by simply printing it out. Now I know you're saying, "I thought this was investing from prison." Yeah, it is, but you must utilize your network and resources to gather all the useful information you need. It's about knowledge and using that knowledge to gain an advantage over the other guy in picking stocks. This book shows you how to be the best, and not come in second! Just because your body is in prison, your brain can exist outside of it.

Yahoo is a good place to go if you have a network of people on the outside that don't mind assisting you. But if you don't, newspapers and business magazines will become your information center. The bible of the stock market is the *Wall Street Journal,* which you can order from the address in the "Resources to Help" section. Last time I checked it cost $98.97 for a 6-days delivery (Monday-Saturday), for 12-weeks.

Be sure to check all current newspaper and magazine rates.

Barron's newspaper is one of the best, and it also lists more stocks than the *Wall Street Journal.* This paper has been around since 1921. A 12-week subscription is $110.97. Next is *Investor's Business Daily.* This is the best for prisoners because it shows charts, stock movement, volume, and 52-week highs, and even has formulas to help you predict where a particular stock might go in the next few days or weeks. This paper comes out once a week and the subscription choices are: 1 day a week for 4 weeks – $33.95; 1 day a week for 26 weeks – $208.00; 1 day a week for 52 weeks – $285.00. Last but not least is USA *Today.* The "money" section of this paper has stocks and useful information on Wall Street. If you're just starting out, I suggest you get this paper, just for financial reasons. A 7-day-a-week subscription is just $75.00.

Magazines are filled with valuable information also. Forbes magazine is one of the financial sector's most resourceful magazines. It breaks down stock, companies, and various investments. You can order from Forbes directly, or from one of the discount broker's accounts. A 1-year subscription is $34.99. Check the "Resources to Help" section to find discount magazine services that offer it for lower prices.

Other magazines that provide valuable information are *Inc., Success, Entrepreneur, Fortune, Bloomberg Business Week, Fast Company,* and *Money Magazine.* You should order all these magazines from the discount magazine people and not directly from the companies. The costs will be considerably less.

Read five newspapers a day. – Warren Buffett

Above are proper steps to succeed, the right way with financial knowledge. Now we turn to how to use that information to pick stocks. Let's start with online brokers, where you can purchase stocks and set up an account with your outside network in less than 5 minutes.

There are many online brokers, but the most important are the discount brokers. In recent years apps have been popping up all over the place trying to court young investors. In my personal opinion, the best is the following:

RobinHood (robinhood.com) – This is a free trading app available for download from App store. It offers more flexibility than using a website. Website trading became obsolete as these new apps became more advanced. This is one of the best apps in the past 10 years.

TDAmeritrade (tdameritrade.com) – This app has free mobile access trading, streaming quotes, real-time balances, funds transfers, and up-to-date news and market research.

Schwab (schwab.com) – This app is from one of the oldest and first discount brokerage firms and offers free trade.

TradeKing (tradeking.com) – With this app you must deposit a dollar to open an account and trades are $4.95. You can also download this app from the App store. You can buy over the counter (OTC) stocks in addition to stocks on major U.S. exchanges. They offer a lot of free trade as well.

Acorns (Acorns.com) – This app connects to a debit card and charges a monthly service fee, which is a small percentage of your account balance. The percentage is based on the amount of money in the account. So, if you leave a small amount of money in your account for a long period of time, the fee could eat your balance. For example, if you only invest $5 and the fee is

20% that $1 fee eats into your balance rather quickly. A $50 balance incurs a 2% fee, and a $500 balance falls to a reasonable 0.2% fee. In a nutshell, the more money put in the lower the fees become.

Motif Explorer (Motifexplorer.com) – This app has a $250 minimum balance and charges a commission of $9.95 for a portfolio that contains 30 stocks and ETFs. It allows users to monitor Motif performance ideas and review performance charts. It can also monitor investment trends.

Firsttrade (firsttrade.com) – This app charges $4.95 per trade and has a stock trading platform with multiple features

IBKR (ibkr.com) – Another stock trading platform app with multiple features; charges $2.95 for trades

All the above apps and websites for discount brokers are for the prisoners who has a network of people on the outside that can assist. My first choice is the Robinhood app, because it's free and easy to use. The founders saw that in order to expand access, they needed to bring in investors with small amounts of capital. These investors, like us, had been locked out of the financial system for decades. In doing this, Robinhood has caused other stock apps to bring down trading prices to compete.

As a first-time investor, the above apps, newspapers, and magazines will help you gain that financial I.Q. that you need before buying your first stock. Because you are in prison you are starting out with one arm tied behind your back, so any knowledge that can be gained should be gained, before moving to invest by picking stocks.

Information is not knowledge. – Albert Einstein

One thing that has bothered me when reading business or financial books is that they were never geared towards the prisoner. Most importantly, instead of getting to the point these authors would include page after page of irrelevant bull crap.

Now, as we move on to making your first purchase, I will not provide bull crap information. Instead, I will quickly give you a step-by-step process that will be brief, with a little follow-up information, so the process is clear. What you must realize is that time is money; eliminate all time thieves, because time is money. You must keep this in mind when trying to gain wealth.

Putting your small amounts of money into work will be what you learn from this book. You are the only one responsible for your financial wellbeing. Remember, no one owes you anything. Don't expect anyone to do the job for you – being prisoners we know this firsthand. My goal is not to show you how to be rich, but to build wealth by investing in stocks. Ownership is everything; that's the way out of poverty and the desperate financial situations we often find ourselves in. So, let's start the process of purchasing some shares.

A prison is indeed one of the best workshops.
– Sidonie-Gabrielle Colette

Chapter 3

Making Your First Purchase

Knowledge is not power, it's only potential power. Knowledge is not mastery. Execution is mastery. Execution will trump knowledge every day of the week. –Tony Robbins

DRIP stands for Dividend Reinvestment Plans. There are more than 700 companies from which you can directly buy stock, thus going around brokers who charge you high fees for their service. You can make cash payments into multiple different plans. These plans and investment vehicle have been around for years, but us as prisoners have been uneducated and misinformed about the process.

Many of you have been told that such an investment was reserved for citizens outside of prison, or that prisoners couldn't do it because of D.O.C. policy. To be frank, D.O.C. has no authority to stop such action, unless you are running a business out of prison. And even that is subject to limited circumstances.

Making your first purchase is easy; the step-by-step process starts as follows:

1. **Stock Picking** – When looking for potential DRIPs, find companies which offer long-term investment choices. Search for strong finances, growth, value, and year-over-year earnings, with strong dividend payouts. (See the following chart with company information, which includes stock names, initial investment amounts, phone numbers, transfer agents, and symbols.)

2. **How to Buy Stocks** – Each company has a transfer agent that you can reach by the phone number next to each company name on the chart. If you have no outside network to help, write a letter directed to the shareholders division of the company, and ask them for their application to join their DRIP program.

3. **Read the Fine Print** – Different companies offer different plans, and all companies listed on the stock market offer these DRIP programs. Some offer no charge of fees, others do. Make sure to ask the company's Shareholder Services Department to provide all the details of their plan, so that you can make the most educated decision on whether to invest.

Companies like CVS Health offer plans that allow you to invest a minimum of $250 into the company without using a broker or fat cats on Wall Street. Remember, you are a small-time investor at this point, so anyway to get rid of the middleman and bring up your cash intake is a plus.

These are essentially "direct-purchase plans," where you can buy stocks like CVS Health (CVS) for a minimum investment of $250 directly from the company. As there are hundreds of companies to choose from, I will only list the most recognized companies and some of the cheapest minimum investments. Check out the "Resource to Help" section for the full address and company phone numbers.

Be miserable. Or motivate yourself. Whatever must be done, it's always your choice. – Wayne Dyer

DRIP Companies

Company	Agent Number	Ticker	Initial Investment
AbbVie	877-881-5970	ABBV	$250
Aflac	800-227-4756	AFL	$1,000

Allstate	800-355-5191	ALL	$500
American Waterworks	888-556-0423	AWK	$100
AT&T	800-351-7 221	T	$500
Badger Meter	877-248-6415	BMI	$100
BB&T	800-213-4 314	BBT	$250
Bristol-Myers Squibb	855-598 -5485	BMX	$250
Brixmor Property Group	877-373-6374	BRX	$100
Caterpillar	866-203- 6622	CAT	$250
CBS	866-595-1717	CBS	$250
Chevron	800-368-8357	CVX	$250
Cincinnati Financial	866-638-6433	CINF	$25
Clorox	800-756-8200	CLX	$250
Coca-Cola	888-265-3747	KO	$500
ConocoPhillips	800-356-0066	COP	$250
CSX	800-521-5571	CSX	$200
CVS Health	877-287-7526	CVS	$250
Dollar General	866-927-3314	DG	$250
Dominion Resources	800-552-4034	D	$40
Domino's Pizza	877-272-9616	DPZ	$65
Dr. Pepper Snapple	877-745-9312	DPS	$250
Duke Energy	800-488-3853	DUK	$250
Eouton	888-597-8625	ETN	$100
EPR Properties	800-884-4225	EPR	$200
Equifax	866-665-2279	EFX	$500
ExxonMobil	800-252-1800	XOM	$250
FEDEX	800-446-2617	FDX	$1,000
Flowserve	800-468-9716	FLS	$100
Frontier Communications	877-770-0496	FTR	$250
General Electric	800-786-2543	GE	$250
Home Depot	800-577-0177	HD	$500
IBM	888-426-6700	IBM	$500
Intel	800-298-0146	INTC	$250
J. P. Morgan Chase	800-758-4651	JPM	$250
Johnson Controls	877-602-7397	JCI	$100
Kellogg	877-910-5385	K	$50
Kimco Realty	866-557-8695	KIM	$100
Libbey	866-252-0125	LBY	$100
McDonald's	800-621-7825	MCD	$500
Microsoft	800-285-7772	MSFT	$250
National Retail Properties	800-278-4353	NNN	$100
New Jersey Resources	800-817-3955	NJR	$100

Nike	800-756-8200	NKE	$500
Oshkosh	866-222-4059	OSK	$100
Pinnacle West	800-457-2983	PNW	$ 50
PNM Resources	877-663-7775	PNM	$250
Quest Diagnostics	800-622-6757	DGX	$100
Resource Capital	877-739-9997	RSO	$100
RPM International	800-988-5238	RPM	$200
South Jersey Industries	888-754-3100	SJI	$100
Stanley/BlackandDecker	888-660-5513	SWK	$250
Staples	888-875-9002	SPLS	$250
Starbucks	888-835-2866	SBVX	$500
Tiffany	888-778-1307	TIF	$250
Tompkins Financial	877-573-4008	TMP	$100
Trust Co. Bank Corp. NX	800-368-5948	TRST	$50
United Parcel Service	800-758-4674	UPS	$250
Valmont Industries	866-886-9962	VMI	$100
Verizon Communications	800-631-2355	VZ	$250
Walgreens Boots Alliance	888-368-7346	WBA	$250
Walmart Inc.	800-438-6278	WMT	$250
Walt Disney	855-553-4763	DIS	$175
Wells Fargo	877-840-0492	WFC	$250
Westamerica Bancorp	877-588-4258	WABC	$100
Whirlpool	877-498-8861	WHR	$250
Yum! Brands	888-439-4986	XUM	$250
Hartford Financial Svcs	877-272-7740	HIG	$50

This list is not a complete list. You will find information in the Appendix on how to obtain an exhaustive list of public companies that offer DRIP buy-ins. These plans must be registered in your name. Follow the instructions to contact the company and ask for a "DRIP Application" and their "Prospectus," which shows the company's financial history. More details will be found in the companies different 'DRIP Packets' about their particular stock and plan options. All these U.S. firms have transfer agents, who you can call over the phone. You contact transfer agents through these websites:

- **Amstock:** astfinancial.com

- **Broadridge:** stockplans.broadridge.com

- **Computershare:** computershare.com

- **Continental:** continentalstock.com

- **Wells Fargo:** shareowneronline.com

Think of these transfer agents as middlemen. Some companies don't have self-administered plans; others have them but still use transfer agents to process the paperwork and stocks being ordered. Go to the website and follow the links to the plans that the agent administers. Some even allow for stocks to be bought directly from the website.

It's important to remember that your dividend is reinvested in more stock in these programs. (The dividend is a reward, usually currency, that a company or fund gives to its shareholders on a per-share basis.) DRIPs use a technique called dollar-cost averaging intended to average the price at which you buy stock as it moves up or down. DRIPs help investors accumulate additional shares at a lower cost since there are no commissions or brokerage fees. And, since these shares usually come from the company's own reserve, they allow you to purchase fractional shares, which are not offered on the stock exchanges.

Some plans allow for you to receive a check every quarter if you don't want to reinvest the money back into the company. But remember that no matter how you accept your profit, it's all income tax purposes. All plans should come with a 1099 form. If they don't, request one from the company or the I.R.S. (see the appendix).

Companies and transfer agents are required to provide cost-basis information; this will help for tax purposes when you decide to unload your holdings. These plans change fast, so be sure you know exactly what is being offered and what you are buying. Remember to request a current prospectus from the company or the transfer agent every six months once you have invested.

Starter DRIP Options

Here are some suggestions for initial investments. The first number is the investment amount you must spend. These are my top picks depending on your current financial means:

$250-level: *Chevron (CVX)* – Chevron is a major oil company whose shares have risen rapidly over the past year. Conflicts around the world have driven oil prices higher. Minimum initial investment is $250

$300-level: *Chevron (CVA) and Disney (DIS)* – Walt Disney is a media giant and just started a streaming service. The CEO has bought all the Disney movies and rights back, so they can only be streamed from Disney Streaming Services. Disney will waive its $100 minimum if you agree to automatically invest at least $50 a month. So, the total amount needed would be $50 dollars, with the other $250 going to Chevron.

$550-level: *Chevron (CVA), Disney (DIS), and Exxon Mobil (XOM)* – Add Exxon Mobil with additional $250. Exxon also offers an IRA (Automatic Investment Service) and has an attractive yield and growth potential for the same reasons as Chevron.

$1,550-level: *Chevron (CVA), Disney (DIS), Exxon Mobil (XOM), and Aflac (AFL)* – If you have $1,550 to spend on stocks, add Aflac, a top-tier insurance company, with a minimum initial investment of $1,000.

$2,300-level: *Chevron (CVA), Disney (DIS), Exxon Mobil (XOM), Aflac (AFL) Becton Dickinson (BDX) and PepsiCo (PEP)* – Becton Dickinson is a top-tier health company and PepsiCo is a consumer-products company.

These reasonable options should help you get started on your quest for financial freedom.

American Depositary Receipt (ADR)

Another option to invest at a discount from prison is through "ADRs" This is international investing made easy and often cheap. ADRs offer dividend reinvestment plans to you also.

ADRs are issued by U.S. banks against shares of international companies, which are held in trust by a branch or other institution overseas. It is important to remember that ADRs are not issued on a share-for-share basis. One of these ADRs may be the equivalent of five or 10 different shares of the company.

Commission rates for ADRs can be smaller than what you would be charged for securities purchased on a foreign market. Your dividends will be paid to you in U.S. dollars and not a foreign currency. For information on direct-purchase ADR plans and to begin the enrollment process, go online to: adr.com.

ADR Companies/Countries
❖ **Argentina**

- BBBVA Banco Frances (BFR)

- Cresud Sociedad (CRESY)

- Empresa Distribudora (EDN)

- Grupo Financiero Galicia (GGAL)

- Irsa Investments (IRS)

- Nortel Inversora (NTL)

- Telecom Argentina (TEO)

❖ **Australia**

- Alumina (AWCMY)

- BHP Billiton (BHP)

- Macquarie Group Limited (MQBCY)

- National Australia Bank (NABZX)

- Novogen (NVGN)

- Sims Metal Management (SMSMY)

- Westfield Corp. (WFGPY)

- Westpac Banking (WBK)

❖ **Belgium**

- Anheuser-Busch InBev (BUD)

- Etablissements Delhaize (DEG)

❖ **Bermuda**

- Marvell Technology (MRVL)

- Nordic American Offshore (NAO)

- Nordic American Tanker (NAT)

- Ship Finance Int'l (SFL)

❖ **Brazil**

- Ambev (ABEV)

- Banco Bradesco (BBD)

- Banco Santander Brasil (BSBR)

- Braskem (BAK)

- BRF (BRFS)

- Companhia Paranaense (ELP)

- Embraer (ERJ)

- Fibria Celulose (FBR)

- Gol Linhas Aereas Intel (GOL)

- Itav Unibanco (ITUB)

- Petroleo Brasilerio (PBR)

- SABESP (SBS)

- Telefonica Brazil (VIV)

- TIM Participacoes (TSV)

- Ultrapar (UGP)

- Vale (VALE)

❖ **Cayman Islands**

- Consolidated Water (CWCO)

❖ **China**

- SI Job (JOBS)

- Aluminum Corp. of China (ACH)

- Baidu (BIDU)

- China Eastern Airlines (CEA)

- China Finance Online (JRJC)

- China Life Insurance (LFC)

- China Southern Airlines (CNH)

- China Telecom (CHA)

- Cninsure (CISG)

- Concord Medical Services (CCM)

- Ctrip Int'l (CTRP)

- E-House China Holdings (EJ)

- Guangshen Railway (GSH)

- Huaneng Power Int'l (HNP)

- Net Ease (NTES)

- Petro China (PTR)

- Semiconductor Mfg. Int'l (SMI)

- Sinopec Shanghai Petro (SHI)

- Soufun Holdings (SFUN)

- Trina Solar (TSL)

- Vision China Media (VISN)

- Xinxuan Real Estate (XIN)

- Yanchoo Coal Mining (YCC)

- Yingling Green Energy (YGE)

❖ **Denmark**

- Novo Nordisk (NVO)

❖ **Finland**

- Metso (MXCYY)

- Nokia Corporation (NOK)

- Stora Enso (SEOAY)

❖ **France**

- Arkema (ARKAY)

- AXA (AXAHY)

- C.G.G. (CGG)

- Flamel Technologies (FLML)

- Orange (ORAN)

- Sangfi (SNX)

- Technicolor (TCLRY)

- Total (TOT)

- Veolia Environment (VEOEX)

❖ **Germany**

- Aixtron (AIXG)

- BASF (BASFY)

- Deutsche Telecom (DTEGY)

- Fresenius Medical Care (FMS)

- Infineon Technologies (IFNNY)

- SAP (SAP)

- Simens (SIEGY)

❖ **Hong Kong**

- China Mobile (CHC)

- China Unicom (CHU)

- CNOOC (CEO)

❖ **India**

- Dr. Reddy's Labs (RDY)

- HDFC Bank (HDB)

- ICICI Bank (IBN)

- Infosys (INFY)

- Wipro (WIT)

- WNS (WNS)

❖ **Israel**

- Delta Galil Industries (DELTY)

- Formula Systems (FORTY)

- NICE Systems (NICE)

- Partner Communications (PTNR)

- Teva Pharmaceutical (TEVA)

❖ **Italy**

- ENI (E)

- Luxottica Group (LUX)

- Telecom Italia (TI)

❖ **Japan**

- Advantest (ATEXX)

- Canon (CAJ)

- Honda Motor (HMC)

- Internet Initiative Japan (IIJI)

- Komatsu (KMTUY)

- Kubota (KUBTY)

- Kyocera (KYO)

- Maki ta (MKTAY)

- Mitsubishi UFJ financial (MTU)

- Nidec (NJDCY)

- Nippon Telegraph & Telephone (NTT)

- Nomura (NMR)

- NTT DoCoMo (DCM)

- Ricoh (RICOY)

- Sony (SNE)

- Toyota Motor (TM)

- Trend Micro (TMICY)

- Wacoal (WACLY)

❖ **Mexico**

- America Movil (AMX)

- Cemex (CX)

- Coca-Cola Femsa (KOF)

- Fomento Economic (FMX)

- Grupo Aeroport C.N. (OMAB)

- Grupo Aeroport Sureste (ASR)

- Grupo Financial Santander (BSMX)

- Grupo Televisa (TV)

- Industrias Bachoco (IBA)

❖ **Russia**

- Mobile Telesystems (MBT)

- Sberbank of Russia (SBRCY)

❖ **South Africa**

- AngloGold Ashanti (AV)

- DRDGOLD (DRD)

- Goldfields (GFI)

- Harmony Gold Mining (HMY)

- Impala Platinum (IMPUY)

- Sasol (SSL)

- Telkom SA SOC(TLKGY)

❖ **South Korea**

- Ericsson (ERIC)

- Svenska Cellulosa Aktielo (SVCBY)

❖ **Switzerland**

- Credit Suisse (CS)

- Novartis (NVS)

- STMICRO electronics (STM)

- Tyco International (TYC)

❖ **United Kingdom**

- Amec Foster Wheeler (AMFW)

- AON (AON)

- ARM Holdings (ARMH)

- AstraZeneca (AZN)

- Aviva (AV)

- Barclays (BCS)

- BHP Billiton (BBL)

- BT Group (BT)

- Carnival (CVK)

- Diageo (DEO)

- GlaxoSrnithKline (GSK)

- Prudential (PUK)

- RELX (RELX)

- Royal Bank of Scotland (RBS)

- Unilever (UL)

- Vodafone (VOD)

These are just a few countries and companies that offer ADR investing on a global scale. Remember to always check the prices, because currency fluctuations will affect the performance of most of the global stocks you invest in. Make sure to check out adr.com to obtain useful information about enrollment. Once you pick a company and get the application, use the SEC website to check all current information. (See the Appendix.)

Before you speak, listen. Before you write, think.
Before you spend, earn. Before you invest, investigate. Before
you criticize, wait. Before you pray, forgive. Before you quit, try.
Before you retire, save. Before you die, give. – William A. Ward

Chapter 4

Stock Picking Points

Being in prison has its setbacks. There is no reason to look at the bad and ugly of the system that is in your face every day. Let's see if we can find a bright side. One of the most positive things about prison is that you have time, time to reflect and slow down. When you were in the streets and you were on the move selling drugs, robbing people, carjacking, and shooting at people for various reasons. So, reclaim your time and focus on yourself.

You have an advantage over people in society when it comes to picking stocks and selling them. That advantage is time. People that do this for a living have to focus on the "every day" of life. You can sit and study all day long, without the distractions of society. Use that to your advantage, study trends, reports, financial data, and newspaper. Learn how to read the charts.

Spend your time looking for stocks that have high earnings and sales growth plus good returns on equity or pre-tax profit margins. Each stock should have an increase in current quarterly earnings per share when you look at last year's quarter for the same period. The greater increase of companies (EPS) is a good sign. Look for the EPS to be up at least 17 to 20% in this year's quarter compared to last year at the same time.

Look for the value of stocks that trade at low prices in relation to profits. Get quarterly Corporate Earning Statements, check the growth rate, and look for annual earnings that have increased each of the past three years. Watching the stocks volume will show a company's supply and demand.

Always invest in the market leader, who has shown strong growth, return on investments, and profits quarter over quarter. Dividend payout is important, look for payout ratio, interest coverage, long-term expected profit growth; three-year dividend growth, and check the yield. These are important keys to success using direct purchase plans.

Many other factors to investigate are IRA options, discounts, improved long and sell options, and stock-secured credit. Since you cannot hold DRIPS in tradition Roth IRAs, look at companies who have put them into their DRIP plans: Exxon Mobil (XOM), McDonald's (MCD); and Wal-Mart (WMT), just to name a few.

Another feature to consider is the discount purchase of shares; usually (REITs) Real Estate Investment trusts do this as well as many utilities. Once you set up an account, you can buy stock weekly, by allowing the company to automatically charge your bank account for shares.

Perhaps the most important feature in these plans is that they are stock secured, where you can borrow money against the value of the stocks you hold. Check plan details because all don't do this, or the company website under "Shareholder Services" or "Investor Relations."

These are all important factors when picking stocks; the goal is to show a net profit. Follow the 3 to 1 ration between where to stay and take profits and where to cut losses. Gains should be 20 to 25%; losses at 7 to 8% of costs cut your ties.

So, you have the basic tools to start out and be successful in your DRIP accounts. Invest in the long-term, support the company's plans with good dividend pay-outs and yields.

Stocks are just the start, my next book will tell you about Venture Capital, investing in companies, and how One Percent has a new tax-free investment vehicle to get around Uncle Sam. This tax-free investment has created more billionaires on transaction than any other tool they have used in a long time.

Part Three:
Buying Bitcoin

Chapter 1

An Introduction

Bitcoin is a digital equivalent of cash, without borders. The Bitcoin technology that underpins it is called the "blockchain," which is the public ledger. Each account on the Bitcoin network, called a "wallet," is put on the public ledger. Every transaction that is sent to the network is digitally signed and a timestamp is made of the transaction. When a transaction is sent to the network, it is recorded on the blockchain forever. This is also known as a "hash," a cryptographical sequence of numbers. Each transaction in this public ledger is verified by the consensus of a majority of the participants in the system. Once a transaction or information is entered on the blockchain it cannot be tampered with or erased.

So that this isn't too technical and math heavy, I will stick to the cryptocurrency aspect of Bitcoin and not delve deep into the blockchain (public ledger). I meant for this book to be short, concise, and to the point, so you have a step-by-step guide to investing, not only in Bitcoins, but also other digital currencies. A cryptocurrency is a form of digital money that uses encryption to verify transactions between peers on a distributed ledger in a decentralized network.

Bitcoin was started by Satoshi Nakamoto, he/she has chosen to be anonymous throughout Bitcoin's rise. We don't know if it's one person or several people working together. Bitcoin was born on November 1, 2008, and the world has changed since its creation. This was followed by a series of transactions on the network to establish Bitcoin as a digital currency. On January 3, 2009, the genesis block was made on the blockchain. January 12, 2009, Satoshi Nakamoto made a transaction, the first of its kind, to Hal Finney.

Under the current system there will be only 21 million Bitcoins in existence. New coins come online when miners solve complex math problems. Each block has 750KB to 1MB worth of transactions.

Recently Bitcoin split into two coins. The developers and miners couldn't agree on a measure to up the processing or powers of the network, so the split created a new coin called Bitcoin Cash – (BCH).

So, whether it's Bitcoin or any other cryptocurrency, you will learn how to track and transfer values from this book. This is no get-rich-quick scheme, just a book of knowledge for interested prisoners. We are closed off from the world physically, but our minds are free to explore, attack our ignorance, and gain knowledge about finances, because it controls our lives in and out of prison. Commissary, phone cards, stamps, lawyer, etc., have become commonplace in our life, but to get an added advantage we must refocus our money on building financial knowledge, investing in the future before we are left behind. What I hope is that this book will help you and your fellow prisoners start investing in the future of cryptocurrency and gain some fundamental business knowledge in the process. So, let's get· started on this quest through this decentralized system.

Bitcoin has three main components: 1) Digital Signatures; 2) Timestamp/Blockchain; And 3) Proof-of-work algorithm.

Things are complex with any investment, then you add the prisoner label to the equation, and you really begin to run up against unforeseen roadblocks. Like with anything that you're trying to learn, you must research and investigate everything pertaining to your subject. This is no different with bitcoins. It may even be more so than typical investments, as you need to research bitcoin as well as other cryptocurrencies markets.

So, the starting point should be to obtain a copy of the "cryptocurrencies" list, which shows all known currencies from the name, ticker, market cap, and price. There are many websites that carry this list, but I personally use https://coinmarketcap.com. Click on "All" and it will allow you to see over 113 pages of cryptocurrencies. You can also see charts at tradingview.com and news about this market at coindesk.com and cointelegraph.com. The proper research will allow you to digest information, spot patterns, and pick when to time your investments.

Chapter 2

Getting Started

Bitcoin is a long-term investment. The bitcoin marketplace doesn't close; it trades 24-hours a day. There are many ways to purchase cryptocurrencies, but the focus of this part will be on buying from what are called "exchanges." This is done by way of a credit card or a bank account. All these companies (to be named) must follow the KYC, "know your customer," and AMC "anti-money laundering," laws that force you to provide information about yourself.

Coinbase

Step 1:   Setup new account

Step 2:   Insert name that can be verified.

Step 3:   Link Coinbase to a bank account, credit card, or both.

Step 4:   Purchase coins by logging into Coinbase and clicking the "Buy/Sell" panel.

Step 5:   Ensure the "Bitcoin" box is selected; a green tick should appear once selected. Type the dollar amount of Bitcoin you want to buy in your currency. The field should read "0.00 USD." Once you have entered the amount, it will show you how many Bitcoins you will be buying. On the right side, you will see blue text confirming the amount of Bitcoin to be purchased. If you agree, click the blue button that reads "BuyBitcoinInstantly" to place your order.

Step 6:   If you don't want to trade Bitcoins then click on "Accounts," click "Send" and type in the "Receiving Address" of your off-site wallet for storage. (More on wallets later.)

The first 5 steps are the most important. I will go into detail about Step 6, storage off-site in wallets, so you don't have to rely on Coinbase wallets to hold your Bitcoins. You've just made your first purchase with Coinbase. Next is Bitstamp exchange, a similar process, but let's go through it!

Bitstamp

Step 1:   Sign up at https://Bitstamp.net, click on "Account," enter your contact details and verify your account by submitting your photo Id.

Step 2:   Connect your bank account, credit card, or debit card. Make the deposit.

Step 3:   Purchase your first Bitcoin by clicking on "Buy/Sell," select "Instant Order" and you should see the option to buy or sell Bitcoin. Type the dollar amount of Bitcoin you want in your currency. Hit "Buy BTC" and you're done.

You must also remember that some of these exchanges will force you to get verified so it's important to have family, wife, friend, etc. use their name to set up the account. Please make sure you keep the account information and password that are used just in case you have a falling out with that account holder. Always use someone you trust.

Other Exchanges
– Bittrex.com

Started in 2014; Co-founder Bill Shihara, worked for Microsoft; List over 257 cryptocurrency coins to trade from; Fast sign up and verification; Easy to create account; Fees: 0.25%.

– Bitfinex.com
Many payment options for funding and unlimited withdrawals; Offers trading in (ii) active cryptocurrencies like Dash, Monero, and Omisego, among others; Uses the charts of tradeview.com, which allows for technical analysis; Also has an App for IOS and Android devices; You need to use Ethereum (ETH) to fund your Bitfinex account.

– Hitbtc.com
Founded in 2013, this exchange allows trading between Bitcoins, Ethereums, Litecoins, Dogecoins, Monero, USDT and more. The exchange also has markets for trading assets, tokens, and ICOs. Trading commissions on Hitbtc are two-fold: Fees: 0.1% and Rebates: 0.1%. Fees are those that you pay, and rebates are paid to you. Also, there are no limits on cryptocurrency deposits and withdrawals, and there are also no fees for deposits.

– Circle.com
Along with Coinbase, Circle is one of the most reputable exchanges in the U.S. The process of setting up an account with them is similar to that of Coinbase.

– Bitmex.com
Online exchange

– Kraken.com
Founded in 2011, it was the first exchange to have its data displayed on the Bloomberg Terminal. Setup is easy, and it allows clients to trade in U.S. Dollars, Canadian Dollars, British pounds, Japanese yen and other digital currencies on their platform.

– Changelly.com
Online exchange

– Poloniex.com

A U.S.-based cryptocurrency exchange that promises to offer maximum security and advanced trading features. It is one of the largest exchanges of all coins in the world, with 100 different cryptocurrency, easy setup pairings. Click the "create your account" button, enter your contact details, set a password, then click "I'm not a robot," click "Agree to the terms of use" and at last click "create account." Poloniex will send you an email to verify your account details. Check your inbox and click on the link provided in the email. Once you're logged in, set up 2-factor authentication for extra security. Click on the spanner icon at the top right and on the two-factor authentication "tab" to begin the security process.

– Cex.io

Buy with Bitcoin, credit card, ACH Bank transfer, SEPA transfer, cash, or Astropay. Purchases made with a credit card give you access to your Bitcoin immediately. The fee is 7%, so $100 only gets you $93 worth of Bitcoin. They also charge 0.2% on trades.

– Gemini.com

Licensed for Bitcoin and Ethereum trading, they have some of the lowest fees. You can buy, sell, and store Bitcoin on their developed trading platform. Purchases fees are 0.25%

– Binance.com

This exchange has landed it owner on the cover of Forbes. The exchange has its own token called Binance (BNB), which you can use to deduct a 50% trading fee temporarily. Regular trading fees are 0.1%. Deposits are free and setup is easy, just e-mail.

Although the above are the most popular exchanges there are several more around the world. The U.S. understanding these exchanges will help in evaluating which one to start with. My opinion would be that you first set up an Coinbase account, because in the beginning you are looking for easy access and setup for your network on the outside.

Investing in cryptocurrencies is a full-time job. Unlike the stock market, which closes at 4:00 pm, cryptocurrency exchanges trade 24 hours a day. Once you manage to fully understand Bitcoins and the other top 50 currencies (more later about the top 50), you can move to altcoins…okay let's slow down just a minute.

If Bitcoin is like Apple Stock, then altcoins are like the penny stocks of the cryptocurrency world. Very attractive, but highly volatile, and only successful if properly researched and timed. People have lost fortunes in their quest to obtain millions. Some have lost millions trying to chase and obtain billions.

Yet people who bought Bitcoins for $10 years ago are multi-millionaires today. The lesson is: you must start somewhere, but wisely. So, starting with Coinbase, I will give you the knowledge and practice you need to start investing.

Interest in cryptocurrency trading is on the rise in prison, since all the newspapers now report it and there are many books on the subject – but none directly geared towards the inmate investor. I watched news segment on CNN one night that showcased an inmate in California, who they called the "Oracle of San Quentin" (that name was hacked from Warren Buffet, the billionaire investor).

This guy featured traded stocks through the phone, with his family members executing his trades on the stock market. Now this brother was sharp, knew his stuff, and had his binder filled with stocks and trades on hand to show the host of the show. Stories like this reveal that inmates have the potential to project beyond the 4 corners of their cell and be successful. Write your own success story; don't let prison officials or other prisoners do it for you.

A fool will lose tomorrow looking back on yesterday.
– Unknown

This fickle market moves fast so you need to get started. Don't be the fool that lives with this looking back at yesterday saying: "I should have invested." For a lot of prisoners, they like to buy commissary, etc., things that have no return on investment from the supplier. When money goes out of your account you should always look for a return of some financial gain. Resources will dry up, family members and friends will stop sending money eventually, so sound investments will allow you to succeed even though you lack the constant finances of the outside world.

There are many reasons to invest in cryptocurrencies. You should have the mindset to buy because:

1. All major currencies grow;

2. My currency updates the maximum;

3. My currency hits around figure;

4. Good news has appeared around my currency

Remember: never take more than a 10% loss in a position.

Bitcoin must be seen in the eyes of the prisoner as a store of value rather than as a currency. The mindset of the prisoner should always be to build wealth, and not as a "get-rich-quick-scheme." Studying and gaining the required knowledge needed to be successful at this will require you to invest in the required knowledge of this market. My booklet is to give you the how-to knowledge on buying Bitcoins, but I can't teach you some get rich quick way to wealth in this field. This is the view of the field from my perspective and some tips to put you on the right path.

Take notice of the different exchanges, so you can pick the one that best fits your trading habits. Grab some cash and get started on your quest for wealth.

Coinbase is the biggest cryptocurrency exchange in the world.

Anything from $20 dollars, $5 dollars, or even 5¢ can be invested. So, this creates avenues for any prisoner to invest and brings the market to anyone.

Chapter 3

Top 50 Cryptocurrencies

The man who does more than he is paid for will soon be paid for more than he does. – Napoleon Hill

Since the first Bitcoin was sold, many have hacked its open-source Blockchain and created multiple coins, like altcoins. These currencies are derived from the core technology behind Bitcoin. At the time of this writing, (2019) Bitcoin had a market cap of $154,796,527,641 and was trading around $8,731 for a single Bitcoin. So yes, the vast majority of the market is smaller than Bitcoin because Bitcoin is the granddaddy of them all. As of June 21, 2019, these are the top 50 cryptocurrencies by market cap:

Name/Ticker	Market Cap	Price
Bitcoin (BTC)	$154,796,527,641	$8,731
Ethereum (ETH)	$28,932,505,688	$272.26
Ripple (XRP)	$19,027,125,759	$0.451772
Bitcoin Cash (BCH)	$8,021,108,775	$450.40
EOS (EOS)	$7,405,229,917	$8.08
Litecoin (LTC)	$7,228,162,486	$116.61
Binance Coin (BNB)	$4,711,423,271	$33.80

BitcoinSV (BSV)	$3,228,556,027	$181.32
Tether (USDT)	$3,129,719,212	$1. 00
Stellar (XLM)	$2,673,654,797	$0.138534
Cardano (ADA)	$2,379,154,633	$0.091763
Tron (TRX)	$2,306,974,895	$0.034597
Monero (XMR)	$1,612,730,842	$94.81
Dash (Dash)	$1,479,132,542	$167.47
IOTA (MIOTA)	$1,411,465,038	$0.507807
Tezos (XTZ)	$1,051,124,390	$1. 59
Ethereum Classic (ETC)	$911,946,452	$8.23
Cosmos (ATOM)	$893,159,150	$4.68
Neo (NEO)	$830,285,298	$12.77
NEM (XEM)	$814,909,880	$0.090546
MAKER (MKR)	$751,608,856	$751.61
ONTOLOGY (ONT)	$741,111,200	$1.50
ZCASH (ZEC)	$566,140,342	$85.29
BASIC ATTENTION (BAT)	$458,134,227	$0.362488
BITCOIN GOLD (BTG)	$437,385,207	$24.97
VECHAIN (VET)	$ 433,456,332	$0.007816
CHAINLINK (LINK)	$429,413,776	. $1.23

CRYPTO.COM (CRO)	$429,079,067	$0.069171
DOGECOIN (DOGE)	$372,151,668	$0.003109
BITTORRENT (BTT)	$365,164,088	$0.001722
USD COIN (USDC)	$360,209,014	$1.00
HOLO (HOT)	$329,728,715	$0.002475
OMISEGO (OMG)	$325,099,973	$2.32
QTUM (OTUM)	$308,130,488	$3.22
DECRED (DCR)	$279,641,813	$28.38
WAVES (WAVES)	$272,996,295	$2.73
LISK (LSK)	$245,125,846	$2.09
TRUEUSD (TUSD)	$234,371,588	$1.00
NANO (NANO)	$232,505,673	$1.74
PUNDIX (NPXS)	$232,266,876	$0.001092
AUHUR (REP)	$224,397,993	$20.40
BITCOIN DIAMOND (BCD)	$205,165,544	$1.10
OX (ZRX)	$202,101,290	$0.33829
RAVEN COIN (RVN)	$196,821,432	$0.054019
DIGIBYTE (OGB)	$192,751,040	$0.016267
ICON (ICX)	$190,687,762	$0.402799
AURORA (AOA)	$189,685,972	$0.028994

BITSHARES (BTS)	$186,713,416	$0.068605
ZILLIGA (ZIL)	$184,687,790	$0.021259
PAZOS STANDER	$170,893,804	$1.00

Source: coinmarketcap.com

At any time, the list of the top 50 cryptocurrencies can be found on the world wide web at coinmarketcap.com

When you look at the above chart the market cap is in the billions, but the trading price is less than $5.00, or sometimes less than a penny. Most cryptocurrencies have many coins in circulation, others have few. As more money is put out there, trading prices almost certainly come down. Remember to do your research because Bitcoin isn't the only game in town. One good website to do this kind of in-depth research is BitcoinWisdom.com. BitcoinWisdom isn't just for Bitcoin research; it allows you to get info on all major altcoins on all the major exchanges.

While we are on this, earlier I talked briefly about Bitcoin and Bitcoin Cash splitting. Bitcoin Cash was born out of some developers wanting to expand the existing Bitcoin trading network. In a nutshell, the main difference between the two is that Bitcoin Cash trades much faster and can trade many times in a short amount of time. What the sponsors hope will happen are fast and cheap transactions.

Things have picked up with Bitcoin Cash in the year and a half since this fork happened. But Bitcoin is still the sexy diamond sitting on top of the hill, because of the trust built over the years. However, being the sexy diamond does come with drawbacks.

So do your research before buying any cryptocurrency listed above. Your goal is to make money, not lose it. The reason you will succeed is because the one thing prison offers that society doesn't is the ability and time to study 20 hours a day. If you configure your time the right way you will be able to build wealth, as I have.

For most of us the TV is the thing that gets the most attention, turning it off and picking up books that expand our knowledge of any given subject will pay off in the end. Developing your investment strategy is the one thing that will pay off in the grand scheme of things.

The only thing that prevents you from focusing on what you want is fear. – Tony Robbins

To start, make sure that you first keep in mind how much money you must invest then spread that money out over different coins. The following is a start-up portfolio, as an example of what your account could look like:

Name/Ticker	Price	Spend
BITCOIN (BTC)	$8,731	$25.00
ETHEREUM (ETH)	$272.26	$25.00
BIANACECOIN (BNB)	$33.80	$25.00
EOS (EOS)	$8.08	$25.00
ZCASH (ZEC)	$85.29	$25.00
LITECOIN (LTC)	$116.16	$25.00

You spend in blocks of $25.00. You receive the equivalent amount of value of whatever the coins are trading at when you buy. Your purchase will appear as a percentage (%) in your account box. So don't think that just because Bitcoin is $8,000 you can't buy it – because you can. Your percentage will reflect what you spend, so the $25.00 will get you a small percentage of a Bitcoin (BTC) or a larger percentage of a cheaper coin. The profit is derived when (if) the value of your coin increases. So, it's up to you to structure your portfolio in the manner that best fits your investment style and the money that you must spend.

Chapter 4

Wallets

Poverty is a powerful motivator. – Unknown

The life of a prisoner isn't easy for several reasons. One way I have learned to make my life easier is to educate myself and rededicate myself to some very good principles. I read somewhere that "rituals, beliefs, and habits cause one to believe that we can control the world," when, we cannot. So just as in life's quest for understanding, we will always need to educate ourselves. The point of this book is to help you in your quest for knowledge and wealth. So, let's begin chapter four about how you can store your cryptocurrency.

There are opportunities, costs, and risk
associated with every decision.

Assuming that you have brought some cryptocurrencies like Bitcoins (BTC), you probably didn't know that you can store them in secure digital wallets. Coinbase, or any exchange, can hold your coins. But if Coinbase gets hacked (they never have), you will lose all of your coins.

Use an online wallet/exchange like Coinbase for small transaction when you are just starting out. For large transactions down the road, I recommend getting a hardware wallet. It will be worth the extra money, once you start moving a lot of coins in and out of different exchanges.

Hardware Wallets provide extra-security by generating a private key on the device itself. Hardware wallets look like USB devices, and you secure the devices further by entering a password to unlock the device itself. Multiple layers of security are the best way to secure cryptocurrency under your control.

Remember, all wallets don't work for every coin, so make sure when picking a wallet, you know what coins are accepted for storage.

Trezor – is a secure hardware wallet with anonymity in mind. There are two models that will hold over 1,000 different types of coins and tokens. They can be purchased from retailers like Amazon or other online stores. (https://trezor.io/)

LedgerWallet – is another hardware wallet. When the idea is for long-term investments in Bitcoin (BTC) use the "Ledger Nanos." It is easy to setup, and you should choose to have a "pin" (personal identification number) to protect you from hackers. Once you begin setup you will be notified of a 24-character seed that will be used to provide you with your private keys. Write it down on a note pad and secure it in a safe place. (ledgerwallet.com)

There are also other options to secure your coins off-site from the exchanges. But listen up – if you are just starting out you should leave the coins on the exchange, because there are costs and fees associated with moving your cryptocurrencies around. Only if you own a significant number of Bitcoin (BTC), should you elect to choose this option. I've included this information to help you along the way.

Two popular Bitcoin (BTC) wallets are **CoinKite** and **BitGo**. CoinKite.com and BitGo.com are easy to set up from their website. While both Coinbase and other exchanges offer web wallets like the two above, the difference is that CoinKite and BitGo put all the security and private keys in your hands for your use.

Another important thing is that if you have a BitGo wallet and choose to buy coins on other exchanges, you don't have to log-in to Coinbase to send Bitcoins (BTC). That means you can send coins directly to those other exchanges at your pleasure. Just know that at the start you should keep it simple. Only once you have amassed multiple coins should you consider this exchange-hopping path with the wallets. What you get from these "web-wallets" is convenience because they are accessible from your family's cell phone or computer. Other options for storage are:

Electrum – this is a desktop wallet only for Bitcoin (BTC). To install on your computer, go to: https://electrum.org/#download. Next, select the version for your operating system and start. Then the install wizard should pop-up. Select "Auto-Connect," and click "next." To keep the default wallet name, click "next," then "Standard Wallet," then "next," or choose the "two-factor authentication" wallet. If you choose this option, the wallet will make you show two different passwords to log in (more secure).

Next you will want to select "create new seed." Click "next" and the wallet generation seed should show up. Grab a blank piece of paper, write it down, and store it somewhere for safety. Click "next," confirm your seed and type it in the box, then click "next" again. Now you will need to make a password to encrypt your wallet keys (make sure it's at least 13-characters long, so that way it's unhackable. The more random the numbers and letters are, the more likely your wallet is safe), then click "next" again.

Now please wait for your wallet address. You should see 3 tabs History/Send/Receive. Receive Tab – you will need to enter on the exchange to transfer Bitcoin into your wallet. Send Tab (Pay-to) – here you enter the address of the person you want to send Bitcoins to. In "Description," add your own notes and enter the amount of Bitcoin (BTC) you would like to send.

Remember, the Electrum wallet is only for Bitcoin (BTC) storage.

Exodus – a software desktop wallet that has a user-friendly design and supports multiple coins, including Bitcoin (BTC), Ethereum (ETH), Litecoin (LTC), Monero (XMR), etc. Also, it encrypts your private keys, transaction data, and tracks the value of your portfolio in real time. You can trade other currencies within their interface using ShapeShift. ShapeShift allows you to quickly swap your coins for other alt coins or cryptocurrencies. This is not an open-source program. (Exodus.io)

MyCelium – a robust wallet for Android and iOS mobile devices. Complete with multiple security features and backups.

CoPay – a robust wallet, great for cryptocurrency users. It is available for mobile devices and desktops.

Blockchain – is an online wallet. Go to Blochchain.info to sign up for a new account.

Block.io – a multi-signature wallet for all Litecoin (LTC) users. Sign up at the above address.

Loaf wallet – a device wallet for Litecoin (LTC). It works on iOS and Android. It is encrypted and can even be installed on your Apple watch.

Jaxx wallet – this is a mobile wallet that supports multiple currencies: Bitcoin, Ethereum, Ethereum classic, Litecoin, DASH, Zcash, and Monero. It also supports eight different platforms: Windows, Apple, Linux desktop, Android, iOS mobile and tablet, Google chrome, and Firefox. (Jaxx.io)

Darkwallet.is – provides stealth addresses and coin mixing, so you can be anonymous while moving coins on and off exchanges.

Atomicwallet.io – is a free multi-asset custody wallet. It can be used for storage of BTC (Bitcoin), ETH (Ethereum), XLM (Stellar), XRP (Ripple), LTC (Litecoin), and over 300 other tokens and coins. It supports AtomicSwaps, a feature that allows users to save on fees and buy cryptocurrency with USD (United States Dollars) and EUR (Euros). Furthermore, the wallet is decentralized with a built-in exchange that allows users to use bank cards.

Breadwallet.com – this is a Bitcoin wallet with easy sending of coins. Users can access their funds more quickly and have full control of their money.

Greenaddress.it/en/ – a Bitcoin wallet that's easy to use for rookies.

Paper Wallets: These are QR code-based wallets that can be quickly scanned, and keys added into a wallet for easy transactions.

While there are currently a vast number of wallets available, the market will determine which stay and which go. So do your research on each wallet, log on to the websites and get all the info printed out of your personal review of these wallets before you buy.

Now that you know the fundamentals of wallets, you can get started on your quest for financial wealth!

For the purpose of trading, consider using Ethereum (ETH) rather than Bitcoin (BTC), because of transfer fees. It's cheaper to buy Ethereum (ETH) for the purpose of exchanging it. Transaction prices: Bitcoin (BTC): $7; Ethereum (ETH): $0.40; Litecoin (LTC): $0.13.

Chapter 5

Other Cryptocurrency Investments

A pessimist sees the difficulty in every opportunity; an optimist sees the opportunity in every difficulty.
– Winston Churchill.

There are many ways to get in the game using digital coins as an investment vehicle. A lot has happened since the start of the Bitcoin explosion. Many companies now accept Bitcoins as a form of payment, and many are developing new ways to implement the "Blockchain Technology" that underpins Bitcoin. Because of this openness and acceptance of Bitcoin, many new avenues to invest have opened to the average Joe.

In this chapter I will show you some new ways to invest using cryptocurrencies. As prisoners, investing services are not available to us. The stock market seems elusive, but we can still invest from our prison cell with the right knowledge (more on the stock market in Part Two). Using middlemen will eat up the little money we have, so doing it ourselves is the only option.

Uphold.com is one potential investment opportunity for prisoners using Bitcoin (BTC). This is one of the best websites for prisoners to setup an account on and invest in precious metal or fiat currencies (*i.e.,* most modern paper currencies, such as the U.S. dollar). Currently Uphold.com has 27 different fiat currencies, precious metals, and four digital currencies: Bitcoin (BTC), Litecoin (LTC), Ether (ETH), and Upholds Coin: Voxelus. Using this avenue opens up opportunities for prisoners with small amounts of income to invest in.

Use someone in your network you trust
to setup the account and get it verified
so trading fees can be waived.

You will be allowed to trade fiat currency, Bitcoins (BTC), or precious metals all from this one website. This will allow you to be a global investor in the precious metal space (*i.e.,* gold, silver, etc.). Instead of buying those chips, snickers, and video games in prison, take some of that money and invest in some gold. For too long prisoners have been locked out of the financial market, only now has it been open for business – so take full advantage of it.

Another website is **BitGold.com**. It's similar to Uphold.com but has fewer options. Still check them both out because one might work better than the other. BitGold also will send physical coins, bars of gold, or silver to an address.

I. C. Os (Initial Coin Offerings)
Another option is I.C.O.s. This is a new form of early investing in companies or ideas put forth by people. Listed below are information and websites that will be useful to you. Do your research because there are scams attached to some of these crowdfunding options.

Before investing money in these companies or ideas with your cryptocurrencies, look for the following and read the fine print.

The Coin/Token "Whitepaper"
This should detail the proposal from the management team. Also, this will be the website's main source of information to the potential investor.

Check Messaging Platform
Usually, these companies or teams set up a slack or telegram page for communication. Here you will find multiple people in communication about the potential I.C.O. of this particular

company. Also check out forums like Reddit.com, BitcoinTALK.com, and STeemit.com.

Resources for I.C.O.'s

tokenmarket.net – This is a marketplace to trade and research tokens and cryptocurrencies. You could launch a crowd sale yourself.

icoalert.com – This site maintains one of the only complete calendars of all active and upcoming I.C.O.s, and token sales.

icocountdown.com – This site features new cryptocurrency projects that will be using crowdfunding.

verifiedicos.com – I.C.O.s

picoloresearch.com – This site offers independent research on blockchain startups and I.C.O.s

cryptosmile.com – This is a blog that contains commentary on the latest I.C.O.'s useful tool

These companies listed on these websites run a pre-I.C.O., which gives tokens to investors before the official crowd sale or I.C.O. goes live. Some of the best investments right now are "pre-bankruptcy" I.C.O.s. Make sure to look at the volume of the coin when the price falls. This might have been said before, but it's important to remember that the falling market is the best opportunity for identifying strong and weak coins and tokens.

When the coin price drops, but the volume does not increase, the coin has no demand.

Another useful place to search is *hitbtc.com*, where I.C.O. tokens appear very fast.

With anything you do, make sure research is done before putting your money in. Take advantage of your circumstances; being locked up allows you to attack your ignorance head on. You have the time to sit down, research and read for hours without the problems regular people in society face. Use this prison experience to build yourself a university of opportunity and let go of your self-doubt. Never believe that prison can stop you from accomplishing anything.

Chapter 6

Other Crypto News Tips

Great spirits have always encountered violent opposition from mediocre minds. – Einstein

I.R.S. and Taxes

Now in 2020, the IRS has put out a new Schedule 1 of the I.R.S 1040 form. This form asks whether you had any transactions in virtual currencies last year, so you now must report them. But you know there is always other ways to get around tax law; the rich do it all the time, so let's use their tactics, shall we?

So, look, crypto currency is looked at as property. So, capital-gains tax on a crypto currency investment is only due when you sell those holdings in crypto. Another move the rich use is selling just your losing positions. That generates capital losses that you can use to absorb gains elsewhere (*e.g.,* stocks). So, using capital losses in crypto currency will help the other position (stocks) when filing taxes.

You only pay if you sell currency, so if you hold on to them, then you don't have to worry about this section of IRS 1040. Also, crypto-currency is exempt from the "wash-rule" that limits capital loss deductions for securities. The rich use these rules to their advantage, so you can too. Please research and obtain the Schedule 1 IRS 1040 (2020) form from irs.gov or write to them; their address is in your library at your institution.

Robinhood App

In the stock section of this book, I will tell you about the Robinhood app as it is used in stock trading. But recently the app has been expanded to investments in crypto currency. It has an exchange and wallet all in one place. The most important thing in trading is that it's free when selling or buying Bitcoin!

There is a downside of sorts, however; you can't transfer coins from Robinhood to another wallet. It's a risk but they have a good security track record with stocks, so crypto will not be a problem. You can find the app on any app store.

Coin Moves 2020

2020 is the year to buy Bitcoin (BTC). In May "halving" will have happened, which will slow production of the coin, create value and an investment opportunity. Another investment opportunity is BinanceCoin (BNB). It recently announced that a new exchange for the currency would comply with U.S. laws, which it has evaded for years, creating a cult-like following. Binance is great to exchange with multiple currencies and its own coin, which is a great value.

CoinBase 2020

Recently, Coinbase allowed customers to move Bitcoin into a personal wallet exempt from know-your-customer and anti-money laundering regulations. This is something that allows you to hold your coins and secure them yourself instead of Coinbase. Also, remember Coinbase sends a 1099-K report to the I.R.S. on trades that exceed 200 or more in one year or a combined $20,000 or more in proceeds. Coinbase has included 25 new coins on its exchange, so check them out at coinbase.com.

Paxful

Some people want to buy Bitcoin in secret, so there are easy ways to accomplish this by logging into Paxful.com. You can find people in your area willing to sell Bitcoins for cash. There is no verification needed, so you can use an alias e-mail address if you want to remain secret.

Bitcoin ATMs

Bitcoin ATMs offer anonymous buys by using cash at the nearest ATM. When it asks you to enter your Bitcoin address, check that you don't have one. This will allow the system to generate a paper wallet for you with a private key and send Bitcoins to your mobile wallet that you installed on your phone, for safe keeping.

BISQ

This is open-source, peer-to-peer software that allows you to buy and sell crypto currencies in exchange for national currencies. There is no registration required to use BISQ. They don't hold your money; it is stored in a multi-signature address rather than a BISQ-controlled wallet.

Covid19

As of this writing, the American economy is grinding to a halt, with unemployment at higher levels than the Great Depression. Covid19 is tearing through the world without caring for anything or anybody. I know this firsthand, because I contracted the virus while being housed at Patuxent Institution in Jessup, Maryland. I fought this thing for 17 days non-stop, and I won the battle. I almost lost my life to a virus, as if I was sentenced to death (I'm not). Across this country I see prisoners dying, getting infected through no fault of their own. Correctional officers and the medical staff that works in these prisons brought death (Covid-19) to our door.

There is a bright side to this: Because of the virus, economic opportunities are open in the crypto-market – the dollar is lagging, and the right coin is rising. When people run away from these markets, that is when you double-down on your investments. Although many prisoners are facing Covid19 at their prisons (Ohio's Marion Correctional Inst. had almost 80 prisoners test positive!) don't lose sight of this troubled time. We are fighters and will always find ways to survive and thrive. Stay strong, wash your hands, and fight. From one Pro Se prisoner to another: Fight!

Chapter 7

Conclusion

Prison takes away everything in its destructive path, seeking to extinguish the human spirit itself. Our name, I.D. number, and prison facilities are different, but our path to prison was probably set in similar circumstances: poverty, underprivileged neighborhoods, and lack of economic opportunities. When I came to prison at age 15, I had no idea this system was holding me back due to where I was born. But I attacked my lack of knowledge with knowledge and fed myself information that filled my brain up and changed my life forever. I always tell fellow prisoners that, "once you have knowledge and know right from wrong, you have no more excuses." So that's what I'm going to say to you – "Pro Se Prisoner" is a mindset that we as prisoners can obtain anything by first gaining knowledge and doing things ourselves; and second by obtaining financial freedom ourselves. Remember, ownership is everything.

Gains reflect behavior,
they are instant feedback systems.
– Unknown

Appendix

Resources to Help

Here will be all the information you need to help you on your travel through the financial world.

Discount Magazine Addresses

- Grant Publication

Box 28812

Greenfield, WI 53228-0812

(Write for catalog, Send SASE)

- Tightwad Magazines

Box 1941

Buford, GA 30515

(Send SASE for catalog)

- TCM Professional Subscription Services

Box 62120

Tampa, FL 33662-2120

(Send SASE for catalog)

- Special needs X-Press, Inc.

927 Old Nepperhan Avenue

Yonkers, NY 10703

(S.A.S.E)

You should order your magazines from these discounted places because they are cheaper than ordering from the company itself. Send an S.A.S.E. to these companies for information, a list of magazines, and pricing details. Some offer one-year subscriptions to 7 or more magazines for as little as $20.

These magazines should help your investing:

- Forbes Magazine

- Money Magazine

- Success Magazine

- Inc. Magazine

- Fortune Magazine

- Bloomberg Business Week

- Entrepreneur Magazine

- Active Trader

- Bloomberg Markets

- Fast Company

Newspaper Information

- USATODAY.com; 1-800-872-0001; $9.99 a month; the best deals are on their website.

- Wallstreetjournal.com; 1-800-568-7625; they have a special online offer: $12 for 12 weeks and $36.99 a month thereafter. Use the website for this deal.

- Barron's.com; 1-800-544-0422; $1 for 8 weeks and 19.99 a month thereafter; the best deal is on the website above.

Dividend Websites/Finances

- seekingalpha.com (free news/option site)

- thediv-net.com (dividends)

- dividends0growth-stocks.com (dividend growth)

- buyupside.com (free dividend tools)

- reddit.com/investing (news)

- yahoofinance.com (financial hews)

- bloombergnews.com (financial news)

- wallstreetjournal.com (financial news)

General Information

- **sec.gov:** The Securities and Exchange Commission has a treasure trove of information available for free public. The "Form & Filings" section and the Edgar System contain all corporate filings and forms that public companies or companies seeking to go public must file. (*i.e.,* annual reports, earning statements, initial public offering forms and reports about changes in business conditions.)

Bonds

- **treasurydirect.gov:** Information provided by the government about how to invest in treasury bonds and other federal government bonds.

- **investinginbonds.com:** Bond information

DRIP Company Addresses

- AbbVie Inc. (NYSE: ABBV)
  1 North Waukegan Road
  North Chicago, IL 60064
  877-881-5970
  abbvie.com
  Pharmaceuticals company;
  Minimum initial investment: $250

- Aflac, Inc. (NYSE: AFL)
  1932 Wynnton Road
  Columbus, GA 31999
  706-323-3431
  aflac.com
  Insurance company;
  Minimum initial investment: $1,000

- Allstate Corp. (NYSE: ALL)
  Allstate Plaza
  2775 Sanders Road
  Northbrook, IL 60062
  847-402-5000
  Property/liability/life insurance company;
  Minimum initial investment: $500

- American Waterworks Co. (NYSE: AWK)
  1025 Laurel Oak Road

Voorhees, NJ 08043
amwater.com
Utility provider/water services;
Minimum initial investment: $100

- AT&T, Inc. (NYSE: T)
208 South Akard Street
Dallas, TX 78202
210-821-4105
att.com
Telephone holding company;
Minimum initial investment: $500

- Avon Products, Inc. (NYSE:AVP)
1345 Avenue of the Americas
New York, NY 10105-0196
212-282-5000
avoncompany.com
Direct seller of beauty products;
Minimum initial investment: $500

- Bank of America Corp (NYSE: BAL)
100 N. Tryon Street
Charlotte, NC 28255
704-386-8486
bankofamerica.com
Bank holding company;
Minimum initial investment: $1,000

- Cincinnati Financial Corp. (NASDAQ: CINF)
6200 S. Gilmore Road
Fairfield, OH 45014-5141
513-870-2639
cinfin.com
Insurance company/real estate;
Minimum initial investment: $25

- Chevron Corporation (NYSE: CVX)
6001 Bollinger Canyon Road
San Ramon, CA 94583
800-368-8357
chevron.com
Crude-oil and natural gas company;
Minimum initial investment: $250

- CBS Corporation (NYSE: CBS)
51 W. 52nd Street
New York, NY 10019
212-975-4321
cbscorporation.com
Media company;
Minimum initial investment: $250

- Bob Evans Farms, Inc. (NASDAQ: BOBE)
3776 S. High Street
Columbus, OH 43207
800-272-7675
bobevans.com
Restaurant company;
Minimum initial investment: $250

- Best Buy Co. Inc. (NYSE: BBY)
7601 Penn Avenue South
Richfield, MN 55423
612-291-1000
bestbuy.com
Specialty retailer;
Minimum initial investment: $500

- BB&T Corporation (NYSE: BBT)
  200 W. 2nd Street
  Winston-Salem, NC 27101
  336-733-3021
  bbt.com
  Bank with 1,800 financial centers;
  Minimum initial investment: $250

- Dollar General Corp. (NYSE: DG)
  100 Mission Ridge
  Goodlettsville, TN 37072
  615-855-4000
  dollargeneral.com
  Discount neighborhood stores;
  Minimum initial investment: $250

- Domino's Pizza, Inc. (NYSE: DPZ)
  30 Frank Lloyd-Wright Drive
  Ann Arbor, MI 48106
  734-930-3030
  dominos.com
  Pizza stores;
  Minimum initial investment: $65

- Dominion Resources, Inc. (NYSE: D)
  120 Tredegar Street
  Richmond, VA 23219
  804-819-2000
  dom.com
  Produces and transport energy;
  Minimum initial investment: $40

- Eaton Corp. (NYSE: ETN)
  Eaton Center
  1111 Superior Avenue
  Cleveland, OH 44114-2584
  216-523-5000
  eaton.com
  Produces components for vehicles, defense, automotive;
  Minimum initial investment: $100

- Flowserve Corporation (NYSE: FLS)
  5215 North O'Connor Blvd., Suite #2300
  Irving, TX 75039
  979-443-6500
  flowserve.com
  Sells precision-engineered flow-controlled equipment;
  Minimum initial investment: $100

- Harley-Davidson, Inc. (NYSE: HOG)
  3700 W. Juneau Avenue
  Milwaukee, WI 53208
  414-342-4680
  harley-davidson.com
  Motorcycle maker;
  Minimum initial investment: $500

- Hartford Financial Services Group, Inc. (NYSE: HIG)
  One Hartford Plaza
  Hartford, CT 06115-1900
  thehartford.com
  Insurance company
  Minimum initial investment: $50

- Johnson Controls, Inc.
  5757 N. Green Bay Avenue
  Milwaukee, WI 53201
  414-524-1200
  johnsoncontrols.com
  Produces automotive systems;
  Minimum initial investment: $100

- Intel Corp. (NASDAQ: INTC)
  2200 Mission College Blvd.
  Santa Clara, CA 95052-8119
  408-765-8080
  intel.com
  Semiconductor manufacturer;
  Minimum initial investment: $250

- Kellogg Co. (NYSE: K)
  One Kellogg Square
  Battle Creek, MI 49016-3599
  269-961-2000
  kelloggcompany.com
  Supplier of cereals and breakfast items;
  Minimum initial investment: $50

- Kimco Realty Corp. (NYSE: KIM)
  P.O. Box 5020
  3333 New Hyde Park Road
  New Hyde Park, NY 10042-0020
  516-869-9000
  kimcorealty.com
  Real estate investment trust;
  Minimum initial investment: $100

- Libbey, Inc. (NYSE: LBY)
  300 Madison Avenue
  Toledo, OH 43699
  419-325-2100
  libbey.com
  Produces glass tableware;
  Minimum initial investment: $100

- Microsoft Corp. (NASDAQ: MSFT)
  One Microsoft Way
  Redmond, WA 98052-6399
  425-882-8080
  microsoft.com
  Software company;
  Minimum initial investment: $250

- National Retail Properties, Inc. (NYSE: NNN)
  450 S. Orange Avenue, Suite #900
  Orlando, FL 32801
  407-265-7348
  nnnreit.com
  Real estate investment trust
  Minimum initial investment: $100

- New Jersey Resources Corp. (NYSE: NJR)
  1415 Wyckoff Road
  Wall, NJ 07719
  732-938-1480
  njresources.com
  Provides natural gas;
  Minimum initial investment: $100

- Oshkosh Corp. (NYSE: OSK)
2307 Oregon Street
Oshkosh, WI 54902
920-235-9150
oshkoshtruckcorporation.com
Manufacturer specialty trucks;
Minimum initial investment: $100

- Pinnacle West Capital Corporation (NYSE: PNW)
400 N. 5th Street
Phoenix, AZ 85072-3999
602-250-3252
pinnaclewest.com
Electric utility company;
Minimum initial investment: $50

- Quest Diagnostics, Inc. (NYSE: DAX)
3 Giralda Farms
Madison, NJ 07940
973-520-2700
questdiagnostics.com
Provides diagnostics testing;
Minimum initial investment: $100

- Resource Capital Corporation (NYSE: RSO)
712 Fifth Avenue, 10th floor
New York, NY 10019
212-506-3870
resourcecapitalcorp.com
Specialty finance company
Minimum initial investment: $100

- South Jersey Industries, Inc. (NYSE: SJI)
  One South Jersey Plaza
  Folsom, NJ 08037
  609-561-9000
  sjindustries.com
  Energy service company;
  Minimum initial investment: $100

- Tompkins Financial Corp. (AMEX: TMP)
  The Commons
  P.O. Box 460
  Ithaca, NY 14851
  607-273-3210
  tompkinsfinancial.com
  Financial holding company;
  Minimum initial investment: $100

- Trustco Bank Corporation, NY (NASDAQ: TRST)
  5 Sarnowski Drive
  Glenville, NY 12302
  518-377-3311
  trustcobank.com
  Regional bank;
  Minimum initial investment: $50

- Valmont Industries, Inc. (NYSE: VMI)
  One Valmont Plaza
  Omaha, NE 68154-5215
  402-963-1000
  valmont.com
  Produces fabricated metal products;
  Minimum initial investment: $100

- Walgreens Boots Alliance (NYSE: WBA)
  200 Wilmot Road
  Deerfield, IL 60015
  847-914-2500
  walgreens.com
  Drugstore chain;
  Minimum initial investment: $250

- Wal-Mart Stores, Inc. (NYSE: WMT)
  702 SW 8th Street
  Bentonville, AR 72716-0215
  479-273-4000
  walmart.com
  Largest retailer in U.S.A.;
  Minimum initial investment: $250

- Westamerica Bancorporation (NASDAQ: WABC)
  1108 5th Avenue
  San Rafael, CA 94901
  707-863-6000
  westamerica.com
  California bank-holding company;
  Minimum initial investment: $100

- CVS Health Corporation (NYSE: CVS)
  One CVS Drive
  Woonsocket, RI 02895
  401-765-1500
  info.cvscaremark.com
  Operates drugstores;
  Minimum initial investment: $250

- ConocoPhillips (NYSE: COP)
  600 N. Dairy Ashford
  Houston, TX 77079
  281-293-1000
  conocophillips.com
  Energy company;
  Minimum initial investment: $250

- Coca-Cola Enterprises, Inc. (NYSE: CCE)
  2500 Windy Ridge Parkway, Suite #700
  Atlanta, GA 30339
  770-989-3000
  cokecce.com
  Beverage maker;
  Minimum initial investment: $500

- Clorox Company (NYSE: CLX)
  1221 Broadway
  Oakland, CA 94612-1888
  510-271-7000
  clorox.com
  Manufactures household products;
  Minimum initial investment: $250

A Complete list of all plans can be found at directinvesting.com

Recommended Reading

- *Directory of Dividend Reinvestment Plans*, by: Horizon Publishing, 800-233-5922

- *Money Master the Game*, by: Tony Robbins

- *Think and Grow Rich*, by Napoleon Hill

- *The Millionaire Prisoner*, by: Josh Kruger

- *Cellpreneur: The Millionaire Prisoner's Guidebook*, by Josh Kruger

Books Coming Soon by C.A. Knuckles

- Pro Se Prisoner: Entrepreneur's Guide to Wealth

- Pro Se Prisoner: The Ph.D. Manual Poor, Hungry and Driven to Success

- Pro Se Prisoner: Alternative Investments Guide to Wealth

- Pro Se Prisoner: Direct Appeal and Post-Conviction Guidebook

- Pro Se Prisoner: Actual Innocence Guidebook

- Pro Se Prisoner: Guide to Challenge Plea Deals

- Pro Se Prisoner: Guide to Correct an Illegal Sentence

- Pro Se Prisoner: Maryland's Prisoner Legal Forms Handbook

Glossary

American Depositary Receipt (ADR): A stock-like security companies outside United States to list their stock in United States.

Annual Income Statement: Summarizes a company's revenues and expenses over a period, either quarterly (10-Q) or annually (10-K). The multi-step income statement includes four measures of profitability: gross, operating, pretax, and after tax.
The income statement measures profitability and not cash flow. Key terms to look for:

- **Total Revenue:** This is often called the "topline," because it's the topline in the earnings statements.

- **Operating Income:** This figure represents how efficient the company is at turning revenue into profits.

- **NET Income:** After operating income, companies have to do a number of things, including pay taxes. Net income, at the bottom of the earnings statement, represents the "bottom-line."

- **Basic EPS and Diluted EPS:** The basic figure, sometimes called the primary figure, refers to the shares outstanding. EPS is the earnings per share, essentially dividing the net income by the number of shares outstanding.

Assets: Everything a company or individual owns or is owed.

Balance Sheet: Listing of assets; shows the financial position of a company at a specific time.

Bear Market: A market in which the value of securities- stocks or bonds, for example-is declining.

Blue-chip Stock: Stock companies known for established earning of profits and dividends.

Bond: A general term for debt instruments.

Bull Market: When the value of securities is rising.

Capital: Money used in business by a person

Common Stock: A class of stocks that are often the ones to receive dividends.

Coupon: Paper attached to a bond; returns to the issuer for payment or interest due.

Crash: A decline in prices, with combined decline in economic activity.

Dividend: A payment issued on a per-share basis to the holder of that particular stock.

Earnings Per Share: Divide the number of common shares standing into the amount left after dividends have been paid.

Equity: The value of property beyond the amount that is owed to it.

Financial Statements: The summarizing phase of accounting. A complete set of financial statements is made up of five components: an Income Statement, a Statement of Changes in Equity, a Balance Sheet, a Statement of Cash Flows, and Notes to Financial Statements. These "notes" can include good information, among them: important statements about various accounting choices, related-party transactions, and information about key business issues.

Fiscal Year: Twelve-month period that a corporation or a governmental body uses for bookkeeping purposes.

Gross Domestic Product (GDP): Total value of goods and services produced in a nation.

Liquidation: The process of converting assets into cash.

Lots: Groups of 100 shares.

Margin: Amount of cash put in when borrowing from a broker.

Money Market: Where short-term debt instruments are issued and traded.

Price/Earnings Ratio: Calculate by dividing the price of a stock by its annual earnings per share.

Prospectus: A document outlining financial and other necessary information for investors to consider before buying new securities.

Real-Estate Investment Trust (REIT): A company that buys, sells, and operates land properties.

Securities: Financial assets.

Yield: Annual rate of return on an investment as paid in dividends or interest.

BONUS CONTENT

Pro Se Prisoner:

The Ph.D. Manual
Poor, Hungry and Driven to Success

Critical Thoughts

We have been told everything about our conditions of growing up in poverty. My goal is to speak to you on the business aspects of growing up poor, uneducated and dealing drugs. Your whole life people have told you that what you were doing was the wrong life, you'll end up in jail or dead. You know all the negative traits associated with growing up in poverty, I will teach you the positive traits of doing the wrong thing, to help you get to the right thing.

Remember, you are ahead of many colleges bound students already, they go to school for 8 years or more to obtain their Ph.D., and you have yours already by growing up in poverty. Ph.D. Poor, Hungry and Driven to Success these three words define your status in the world. How you use these street traits is up to you, but let's be honest we all use them to justify selling drugs to our own people as if blacks in the ghetto is the reason you have your problems of growing up in poverty.

Take for instance: drug dealers. Your businessmen without even knowing it yet. You have started a company, albeit drugs, but still a company. You have taught yourself accounting supply and demand, and marketing without going to school for Business or obtaining an M.B.A. from an expensive Business School. Now, take what you learned in the streets about business and apply that same hustle to doing something legal and you will obtain fortunes the corrupt streets and drug dealing can't offer you.

[P]: Poor

As a black man above, the odds are stacked against you at birth, depending on your social security number, zip code, and city and/or county you were born in. I'm from Baltimore city, the most corrupt city of this era; multiple mayors, city council men and women and multiple police have been convicted, imprisoned, and put out of office. I sat in my prison cell and thought out loud, why do the citizens of Baltimore keep electing these people to office? These are black leaders doing this to black citizens year after year to no avail.

So, I looked at some numbers, and they showed some devastating things. Almost half of Baltimore's adult population does not have a job. Wow! half that's over 250,000 people without a job. Fifty percent of Baltimore's black men are under some form of the criminal justice system. That's prison, jail, parole, or on probation. Fathers are gone out of children lives. Faced with these numbers, we fall and never have a chance to take a step forward. My goal is to pull you up the mountain, even if that means you will be screaming, kicking, and crying your way up.

Being poor is a humbling experience, you learn lessons, and are shown things you otherwise wouldn't learn if your parents had money to shield you from this dark corner of America. But to understand poverty you must look back in history and see the deliberate attempts that turned many good neighborhoods that once flourished with good jobs and money, into hell pits of drugs and crime ridden projects, with no jobs or upward mobility.

Baltimore knows this story all too well because the Cherry Hill Projects, was the first suburban-style planned community for African Americans; this was residential segregation by design in the U.S.A. at its best. There weren't any basic things there that would normally be in a new neighborhood. Schools, grocery stores, and a shopping center were nowhere in sight.

But once again, when the government tried to dismantle, we were poor, hungry and driven (Ph.D.) and saw the opportunity to set up our own stores, drugstores and grocery stores. Instead of a store front we developed the first Uber Eats and Grub Hub, by using old trucks and fitted them to hold food, household items, and drugs (legal), to have these driving around every impoverished neighborhood to make up for the lack of infrastructure and stores in the early 1930's-1960's. Out of dismay we created opportunity. Baltimore had many shipyards that attracted people to the city; this was home to the SS Frederick Douglass Ship. These were high paying jobs, that in tum allowed many blacks to open stores, such as bread companies, grocery stores and drug stores in their neighborhoods. We succeeded at this time because of we were held down and segregated by our own government, one of our most promising figures was "Little Willie" Adams, who financed scores of black businesses, but help start Super Pride grocery chain and Parks Sausage Co. If you grew up in a inner city you know these two stores as Staples in the hood, but you probably didn't know it was started by a Black man, from Baltimore. From grocery stores to Banking with William March, who co-founded Harbor Bank of Maryland, the state's first-owned black bank.

Baltimore was built on the backs of Blacks that came from the south, who started churches, businesses; worked at the mill, railroad, factories and the likes, which in the early 1830' s was prime time pay. Reconstruction gave blacks hope that they finally reached the promise land. There were planned efforts to keep blacks in slavery, not physically in chains, but mentally and financially by deny basic rights that created poverty; some important things to remember about Baltimore, and Maryland at-large was that segregation still existed. Maryland rejected the 15th Amendment, guaranteeing voting rights to African Americans.

(1870) Maryland School of Law in Baltimore Banned African Americans from attending. (1891) Baltimore enacts the nation's first housing ordinance segregating neighborhoods. (1910) Maryland even passed a law in (1924) to punish any white women who had a child by a Blackman. Remember, Freddie Gray was not the first Black-person killed by police; this was going on in (1942) when Pvt. Thomas Broadus-a black soldier was killed unarmed by police. The 14th Amendment wasn't ratified in Maryland until 90 years after it was passed. (1959)

So, when you think that this system wasn't planned and plotted, history tells us another story that shows that it was. This system was created long ago, but "Jim Crow" was legalized by the U.S. Supreme Court decision in Plessy V. Ferguson (1896), which made the "separate but equal" law, the law of the country. Then came one of the most effective financial decisions that to this day Black people can't crawl out from under and is the one policy that kept generation after generation in abject poverty and improvised neighborhoods. That financial policy was: "Redlining", this was when the U.S. government/banks decided not to offer loans and assistance to the poorest neighborhoods deeming them beyond help. Most poor neighborhoods were redlined into poverty on purpose because black residents lived there. Houses were torn down, and massive housing projects were developed in their place. Black poverty was planned. The government and private business created the conditions · and roadblocks that allowed poor black neighborhoods to exist for multiple decades, even today these conditions are still in place. As Chris Wilson, author ·of the "Master Plan" stated: "Society put obstacles in the way of black people-slavery, lynching's redlining, and job discrimination, voter discrimination, and all manner of segregation, official and otherwise-then criticized us when we didn't rise above it."

The U.S. was creating a middle-class but was also excluding people at the bottom from gaining financial freedom merely because of their race: Black! As Frederick Douglass said: "Knowledge is the pathway from slavery to freedom." This is the start of the pathway from which you will have the knowledge to unchain your mind from mental slavery and drug dealing to business owner and free member of society, that controls his/her own destiny.

There are too many black millionaires and billionaires, for our people not to have the resources at the bottom of the chain to set their self-free. One of the problems with black people is that we look at each other as enemies and an adversary. So instead of reaching out to help, we see a threat, we have been so mind fucked by slavery, Jim Crow, and segregation, that someone that looks like us is looked at as a foe instead of a friend. Growing up in Baltimore I had the same thoughts, walking down Edmonson Ave, in West Baltimore, I thought the black person walking up the street wanted to do me harm, because that's all I knew, I was uneducated, lost, stupid, and a victim of not being taught that this lack of opportunity was created long before I was an egg in my mother's wound. This system was developed generations before me, so my view around my 4 corners of my block obstructed my view of the bigger picture. That we looked at each other as threats because that's what the system was designed for: abject poverty, with no ladder to climb out. Even black mayors, councilmen and women, prosecutors, police, and state legislature members supported these destructive policies that have not only destroyed thriving black communities, but that has ultimately sustained poverty in our community's generation after generation.

Instead of these successful black members of the elite class, creating local neighborhood wealth, they have sat on the sideline. When they should have been descending back into these poor neighborhoods and sharing knowledge and resources, they have become enlightened and ascended past their own brothers and sisters. I choose to stand on the front line and share knowledge, to free my people and the white poor from their mental bondage and allow them all to have financial freedom, show them the way out. Knowledge opens doors and cures the evils of poverty.

Black people's spending power is a trillion dollars. That's power along, use it to weld change. Together we will look at the high violence and high unemployment as an opportunity to become investors of the poor people. Instead of yelling and telling guys to get off the comer or go to prison, try instead to: "Listen and Ask" them question about what they want and how can you help them achieve your goals? If you ask questions and listen you can have a better conversation, the years and choice of threats and prison have fell on deaf ears of the businessmen of the streets. Change the approach, get a different result.

Jobs are essential to change these environments, for years Baltimore has disinvested in poor neighborhoods, only to keep building downtown Baltimore up as a model. Equally efficient redlining policies are still in effect today. Take Bohon Hill, in the 1900' s it was wealthy but relinked during the Depression. Knowing the past you will understand the future, these policies are nothing new. As part of the "New Deal" in 1937 the U.S. created the Homeowners Loan Corporation (HOLC), this law rated neighborhoods as "declining" or "undesirable". You would think that these areas were poverty stricken or crime ridden, but no, these were designated as "declining" simply because of the threat of the "Negro" population in these neighborhoods. Based on those rating systems by the governments banks wouldn't give loans to people in these areas. This caused housing prices to drop, this created poor, black ghetto's that still exist today all from the 1937 New Deal Law that was passed by the U.S. government. No neighborhood affected by this law has ever recovered to this day.

Another thing that has created poor neighborhoods and people is mass incarceration.   Five percent of black men in their twenties in Baltimore are in prison or parole/probation. Every black person that has grew up in Baltimore, lived in Baltimore or still go to Baltimore (People who moved out) have or know someone that's locked-up. My goal is to give these citizens that people have written off an opportunity to use the mental power to obtain success. There is too much financial upside to help these citizens, then to leave them in poor, crime ridden neighborhoods.

Politicians want to just lock citizens up, without fixing the "underlining" problems which are "financial literacy" and opportunity to climb the ladder to success. We have incarcerated the men out of these neighborhoods to no avail, we have 2.2 million people locked up in this country over 5.5 million counting parole and probation. This isn't working, so the policy needs to change, and Blacks need to stop supporting this approach. Why not help the hustle start a business, because for too long we haven't funded or gave money to these neighborhoods for this. I was told that: "Hustlers are entrepreneurs without capital and knowledge to succeed the correct way." Mostly, hustlers can't look around the comer because their view is blocked by an imaginary wall, that tells them it's danger over here don't come. Feeling comfortable with their life they stay around the comer hustling. If all you know is that comer, it's hard to leave that corner. I will support you and give you the knowledge to step around that comer. Even innocent kids get trapped behind this wall.

Once you return to society there should be resources to help, a job, a place to stay, and someone that will mentor and show them the ropes. This system of Criminal Justice has been created to wreak havoc on the poor. It shows privilege to those with wealth, power, and race (white) to determine how fair it will be to those that break the law. So, we must oppose this corrupt system, and not sit on the sidelines.

The courtroom is the place where citizens see their government at work You Vs. U.S.A., this is where you see if you have those rights the constitution says every citizen supposed to have. Forget what the Constitution says, see what the Constitution does through its action on ordinary citizens. Prison allows reflection, it's a place meant to break you down, mentally, and physically, it's a place where you lose everything, except your desire to change. Some people have it sealed up, others act on it and open it up, but you don't lose that desire to change, you just need the knowledge to act on it. So, mass incarceration plays a role in poverty. If we want these citizens to return to society rehabilitated and educated, so they won't put a strain on resources of the poor, we need to help rehabilitate these citizens while they are in prison, so upon release they can successfully integrate back into these neighborhoods and help build them up, instead of breaking them down.

Sending uneducated, skill lacking, improvised citizens out of prison, you create a cycle of poverty to prison; and a cycle of poverty to parole/probation, that creates continued poverty and mass incarceration. Democrats created mass incarceration, and Republicans monetized it, and allowed private contractors to charge prisoners and their families over the top prices, just for millions in kickbacks from these companies. So, what allies can you rely on to help you as a prisoner achieve your goals? You! Once you realize you can do more with your life than sit in prison, once you realize that educating yourself is the first step of breaking the cycle of poverty and mass incarceration, you will see you need no one but yourself. It's your choice alone, to progress in prison and to be successful outside of prison comes down to choose. You may be locked behind the wall, but you still have control over your actions, thoughts, and how you live your life while inside. As Brother Malcolm X said: "where else but in a prison could I attack my ignorance by being able to study intensely, sometimes as much as 15 hours a day." Brother X was correct, prison can teach you to attack your ignorance of not knowing that poverty for you was planned; mass incarceration was planned for you and people who look like you; Income inequality was planned. Drugs destroying our neighborhoods were planned by the CIA to fund a war in South America, once that torch was lit, the black drug dealers, was unknowingly being complicit in a government-controlled system of a racial exploitation. This system was developed and helped along the way by Black politicians who would get tough on crime. Several Black leaders we held up high in the sky supported mandatory min. sentence. One was Asst. District Attorney named: Johnnie Cochran, yes, the one who represented O.J. Simpson. At the time Cochran was the first black Asst. District Attorney in the country. Instead of destroying this system of racial exploitation, he supported getting tough, which included: judges handing out longer-sentences for drug offenses, up to the maximum sentence in some cases. Drugs were a direct result and symptom of poverty, both direct results of a planned government action. Local city mayors have done their part also to help the U.S. become the largest jailer of its people. Every choice, decision made, or reaction to a national crisis has built this prison industry complex year-after-year for the last seven decades. Then came the federal war-on drugs during in poor neighborhoods. In response to it, in 1984, 1986, and 1988, the length of sentences was increased under the mandatory minimum guidelines. Both Black and White, Democrat and Republican, was eager to set these drug sentences high, thinking it would stop the selling and using of drugs. Then came the dumbest policy in the War on Drugs history: hundred-to-one-cocaine-to-crack ratio. Let's be honest this was because Blacks sold crack and Whites used powder cocaine. This was legal racial discrimination in the criminal justice system, one that had been fought over for decades to no avail.

For many, a criminal conviction makes it out right impossible to vote, find a good cost-effective job, and housing. So, the effects on people who are already poor are severe, but remember criminal justice doesn't forgive, it destroys your life in prison and once released with parole and probation. There is more than one way to skin a cat. For instance, while we fight mass incarceration, we get caught up in the "hot topic" of the day (i.e., mandatory min. sentences), when other things slide under the radar, like the 1994 federal crime legislation that allowed unlimited federal dollars to fund the constitution of prisons across this country, this happened under President Clinton. Clinton was the President that did the most to create mass incarceration; it's his policies that continued Regan legacy, and the housing policies of the New Deal under FDR, that created "Redlining" by banks. While drug dealers sell drugs, that is a symptom, of the problem which was government policies that created poverty and mass incarceration in the first place. One in four black men was caught in the continued cycle of the criminal justice system. From slavery to Jim Crow, to mass incarceration.

My last point in the education of why these poor neighborhoods were created, and the role mass incarceration played in it. About twenty percent of America's prison population is locked up for drug offenses. This new Criminal Justice reformer, which came to this party late, likes to hold-up these "low-level" drug offenses as the end-all-be-all of mass incarceration reform. But I like numbers, so let's question this false narrative and focus on the facts for a moment. You can let go of all of these "low-level" drug offenses citizens in federal and state prisons, and we will still have the highest prison population in the world! Don't get caught up in the hype· that President Obama, President Trump, and all the politicians around the country tell you because, that's not the reason why America has the highest prison population in the world. Then, on top of that "low-level" drug offenses don't even account for the vast majority of drug offenses of incarcerated citizens with drug offenses.

Moreover, violent crimes or offenses make up fifty three percent of this country's prison population, and a vast majority of these violent offenses were committed by juveniles and citizens between 18-24 years old. With Maryland the state I reside in coming in second for incarcerating this age group. These were the suppose "super- predators" of the 1990 's, the lost forgotten people of our society. According to the Bureau of Justice statistics in 1980 the prison population was 329, 122, as the War on Drugs, housing policies, crime bills, etc., came in the 80's and 90's, the prison population skyrocketed to 2.3 million as of today. Recently, the Trump Administration passed the first step Act easing drug-related mandatory minimums sentences, the jury is still out on the effectiveness of this law, but it's a start, many people were released and I'm happy that, at least they can get back to their lives and create opportunity for others.

Solving the issue of mass incarceration will reduce the strain on taxpayers. At the costs of about $40,000-$50,000 to house a prisoner, you could educate and send to college for $4,000 a year. These will enrich lives and not destroy them. Our system of criminal justice contributes to poverty and burdens the poorest among us the most. It's just a link in the chain that ultimately needs to be broken down.

As Clarence Darrow addressed in 1902: "If the Courts were organized to promote justice the people would elect somebody to defend all these criminals, somebody as smart as the prosecutor-and give him as many detectives and as many assistances to help and pay as much money to defend you as to prosecute you.

Another example of the constant struggles of the poor and how this was planned is the often-unregulated industry of: Pay-day loans, Rent-to-own, Cash Advances, Title Pawning, and Tote-the-note car lots. These places are in every improvised neighborhood and poverty-stricken region of this country. Believe me this is not by accident, this was a thought-out plan by this industry, who fed lies to these communities that they were helping lower income people succeed. But in reality, they were ripping off these citizens. With such schemes as "predatory lending", which in essence kept people in poverty, and at the bottom of the economic ladder. This industry was brought about because of the "redlining and other Big Bank decisions that were in place, that didn't lead to people being in poverty. So, these money men would raise the interest rates above I00% because traditional banks wouldn't lend to them, so predatory lending was established. Why do you think that these "lenders" are located only in improvised neighborhoods? Rich people won't pay them, and often it's the rich that have been allowed to operate these "poverty generating machines."

Citizens that use these "lenders" should stop now, you have been given this false sense of financial stability, only to later realize that you were wronged somewhere along the line. You will face more debt, cars lose, evicted from Section 8, etc. the majority of people that use these services, never pay the interest back on the loan, which can exceed over 100%, if the Big Banks believe that you can't pay back 2.0%, why would you pay back 90.9%? These companies know that it's high risk, but it's a good financial move for them because you will forever be in debt with them, and they can sell your debt with interest to some other entity. An informed citizen can see the scam, so this book is to educate you on these tactics used to keep low-income people at the bottom, as a relied upon min. wage work force. In the past 30 years the cost-of-living inflation has risen, but not until a couple of years ago has the min. wage increased. Even the $15-a-hour raise is not compatible with the rising cost of living and inflation. This is the knowledge of these industries, government, and financial institutions that have executed these plans for decades, blocking change at every step. My goal is to empower you with the knowledge, because "once you know, there are no more excuses." All these improvised neighborhoods, incarcerated citizens, and people of black and white race who have been the forgotten people and who are in desperate need for help.

This is your start at understanding why these communities exist in every state, city, county, and country around the world. The U.S.A. is the richest, most powerful nation in the world, but hasn't fixed this poverty problem in America, but gives resources to other countries to fix their problems with poverty. So, this is the reason why, because they don't want to fix it, they want to place a patch here, a patch there, just to keep this valuable resource of humans at the bottom. I will attempt to explain to you how the rich act, so you can understand how the rules are different and how you may be able to use them in your life to obtain financial freedom and a ladder out of poverty. Remember, poverty means the state of one with insufficient resources. This manual will be your guide and resource out of poverty.

[H]: Hungry

When you eat food, you become full, but when you are hungry your stomach growls, make noises, and it seems as though you can't focus because of these strange feelings. You desire food to subdue t e hunger pains. Our lives growing up on food stamps and public assistance, put a hunger for money and a way out of poverty in our stomachs, but only if we had the proper knowledge (food) to feed these stomach pains we would have learned early on how to navigate the legitimate avenues that could provide real financial freedom and not the illegal entrepreneurship we instead took up. We were ignorant and blocked from these avenues that could help us climb out of poverty. The ghetto gave us hunger, but not the knowledge (food) to feed our desire, drive, and purpose. We never were taught what to do with money, so we spent it, once that was gone, we needed more, and more so we start selling more drugs, killing for it, and even robbing people to obtain money. But it always went back to the same feeling of needing more, because as soon as we got it, we spent it. Not knowing how to spend, invest, and by assets, we continued to sell drugs to get ahead only to feel incomplete, because the desire to get ahead was there but the lack of knowledge (food) alluded us as to why we never had money and why we spent it faster than we received it? What we didn't see at that time was that we thought that money was needed to make money. Our belief was that we needed it to sustain our lives, but that's wrong. We had all the things we needed but didn't have the knowledge to put them together as one. We needed a brain, the ability to read, and your thoughts/imagination. The limits of your brain are only limited by you, no other force of economics can limit it. So, as you dream, and conceptualize, so you become. We had learned all the way to obtain money and end up dead or in prison. We learned all the ways of robbing people for money or killing for money. But never was educated on legitimate purposes of Business, Money, or long-term Financial Freedom. So, to teach you how to direct your "Hungry" into real assets and financial freedom, I will teach you the rich think and what they teach their heirs. This will be your study guide of poverty.

Ignorance will cause pain and poverty. Having knowledge without action will only allow you to continue dreaming. First, always make sure to remember that poor people spend all their money, while the rich invest theirs. Your expressway to financial freedom should start with the above quote then secondly, remember your own! Own! Own! Never be deaf, dumb, or blind. Open your eyes, the rich don't have jobs, they own companies, stocks, and your debt. Why go to school/college for 4 years go into debt with student loans, only to obtain a master's degree, but owe your future work income to the debt collectors for the Degree you sweated four to eight years for. College creates the work force for the rich, while the majority of wealth is created by the middle class, not the rich. The rich own the wealth created by the middle-class. Sitting in prison, you have the time to study and conquer what people in society try to do while in 4-year colleges: "gain knowledge, and act on it." What you own determines who gets rich. The rich use businesses and investing to achieve this feat, and so can you. There is no need to be mad at the rich for using their money to lobby for better taxes, and low interest rates for loans.

I have read many financial books over the years but Tony Robbins' "Money Master the Game" had the most impact on me. It's like what Napoleon Hill did back in the day, when he interviewed the 1%ers aka the rich and showed you, their strategies. But there are five strategies called V2MOM that's in the introduction by Marc Benioff (founder and CEO of

Salesforce.com), that summed up my vision or this manual. Here are the five questions:

1. What do I really want? (Vision)

2. What is important about it (Values)

3. How will I get it? (Methods)

4. What is preventing me from having. It? (Obstacles)

5. How will I know I am successful? (Measurements)

So, please answer the above five questions from Tony Robbins (V2MOM) and start your quest for quality financial freedom. Every time you embark on another goal re-write your answers to the above questions, so you can have a different perspective going forward. Let's all end the rat race and start and fulfill our financial dreams. The rich are successful because of several things like opportunity, education, financing, taxes, ownership, etc. but these successful people always have left clues and footprints along the way, we have never studied these steps as poor people, and especially haven' t as prisoners. We are taught to despise these people. Instead, we should study these people and learn and grow from the mistakes they made and learn how to become successful ourselves. Growing up in poverty we have developed certain traits that people outside of the poverty-stricken ghettos don't have, so we break norms all the time. Our hunger comes from depleted resources, lack of proper education, and being systematically deprived of upward mobility. So, out of that exclusion from normal society, we go to use underground means to gather economic relief. Remember, this wasn't always the case we had a chance during Reconstruction, in Tulsa, Oklahoma, in 1921, dubbed "Black wall Street," because of the entrepreneurship and success of this black section of Tulsa. While society, with their guns and explosives destroyed the wealthiest black community in the nation. We have shown that if you give us a chance we will fly past all obstacles in our way, that community in Tulsa represents success and that threatened societies in America, so it had to be burned down. Our ideas, performance, money, success, and our land were looked out as disposable. We must get out of the mindset that it's only three ways to success and out of the ghetto: hustling, hip-hop, and hoops. Tulsa shows that when opportunity is given to citizens in poverty, they will soar above all the limits and barriers in their way.

"To be yourself in a world that is constantly trying to make yousomething else is the greatest accomplishment."

-Ralph Waldo Emerson

My whole life people said I was smart beyond my years, a A-student in school, the problem was that giving up in poverty didn't offer me the proper education, to allow me to challenge my intelligence, so while I knew I was different I used that knowledge to sell drugs and out smart people in my neighborhood, so why I had sparks of genius, I had no platform to explore it. So, because I didn't have opportunity, and a place to challenge my intelligence, as a kid, my goals turned to the streets, trying to create opportunity; but not seeing that my hunger to get ahead was destroying my neighborhood and the citizens that already had nothing. My dreams now are to feed the hunger of the streets with knowledge and teach them how to master their own terrain (entrepreneurial), and how to recycle and reinvest money back into their own neighborhoods, that's legal and leave the drug trade alone. Although we try and some fall short of changing and making it out, we still must try to defeat these opposing forces that distract and promote the destruction of our neighborhoods. Your hunger was molded from the lack of opportunity and access to respectable financial means. You survived in a cop-infested business while looking over your shoulder for killers and robbers. But you gained a sense of business from those illegal transactions, you learned accounting, you even developed marketing skills that separated your product from others.

Developing these skills is good, but what the streets didn't teach you was financial literacy, and how to invest in legit businesses. The rich teach their kids differently about money; their schools teach financial literacy and the basics about money. Section 8 and Welfare are traps for people in poverty. Knowing you need assistance these programs provide a crunch in times of need but suck you in for years and even sometimes for generations. The sole purpose of a security blanket like Section 8 and Welfare was to protect those in improvised conditions by offering assistance. Instead of providing jobs, training, and a chance at upward mobility, these programs trapped many citizens in poverty for a lifetime. No person has hunger, you have to grow up the way you have, that's why I want to share this knowledge to let you have the system and your strengths so you can plan a better future. Most important thing is your "Plan", write it down on paper it's easier to follow when you can see it in front of you.

Credit is King, and you can build this even while in prison. There is a website called www.creditstrong.com that allows you to spend $15-50 a month on $500, $1,000, and above lines of credit. You pay $15 a month until the $500 is paid back, and then you get the actual $500 dollars, but the important part is that you get 120 transactions on your credit report, which accounts for the payment history, this way you're always on time. You can sign a financial power of attorney over to someone you trust, and they can set it up for you. Believe me, the rich have mastered credit, that why the big banks love doing business with them, you are one's the banks "redlined" out of banking, housing loans and business loans. Why could they lend to someone on Section 8 and Welfare? That's how they think about us in poverty-stricken areas. My goal is to give you their secrets, to help you out of poverty and hustling. Now, your plan is first, write it down; second is building credit (check-out website); thirdly, this book is the motivation and background to give you the history of the problem and showcase the power you have built in your system just by growing up in poverty. Odds stacked against you; you succeed; placed in improvised ghettos; you use that as a driven force to step out of those slums. The system put you in those ghettos and just like a magician pulled a slight of hand and tried to put so many drugs, poverty, death, and vengeance before you to block you from seeing the great opportunities and what's possible beyond those ghetto walls. Mass incarceration took or rather stole fathers from kids, those kids in tum did the same to their kids, which left 3 generations behind bars, when effectively took income out the home, and left grandmothers to raise multiple generations of kids, again draining resource and income in the process. All the while building hunger inside and. that drive. All of which came from growing up poor. This is the start of being able to use your Ph.D.

Remember when the magician used the sleight of hand trick right in front of your face? You looked out and saw big time drug dealers and expensive cars; that illusion blocked what's possible and denies the viewer ("You") from seeing the opportunities; thus, not knowing such opportunities exist, that will allow the Ph.D. Poor, Hunger, and Driven to Success to succeed and remove them from the ghettos that enslave them. The viewer ("You") sees drug dealers, pimps, fiends, and ghetto walls that go on forever. That lack of exposure to see past the magician, blocks the view of Wall Street, Doctors, Scientist, and Fortune 500 businesses, that will show you how successful businesses are run and, in tum allow you to make your own capital and start your own business, to rise out from under the magician's illusion that has shown you nothing but poverty.

Throughout history we have always been driven, born out of slavery and poverty. But every advancement was followed by a backwards regression of the previous advancements. Things like abolitionist getting President Lincoln to bring enslaved blacks into the Union Army; then Andrew Johnson took it back. Black Wall Street in Tulsa during pre-desegregation only later to be burned to the ground by whites. Before the 1930's, black owned houses and land, since the 1930's homeownership has fallen for blacks. What has happened? To answer this question and uncover the magician's tricks, we must first identify what the challenge was then, and what it is now? So, what's the challenge that we have to overcome? Over the years many programs have popped up and foundations exist to fight against poverty but post- desegregation poverty in the communities is at all-time highs. 43.5% of the population is poor; 2% of the population controls 80 to 90% of the wealth this nation creates. So, the challenge I have identified is: There is and never has been a full throttle advancement of an economic agenda put forth. That deals with the Black home ownership decline, and lacks diversity in government contracts, etc. the old guard that did sit-in, protested, and held peaceful marches, also must be held accountable for their failures that have costs generations of Blacks and people of color to further fall down the economic ladder. So, before you picked up the drugs to sell; before you shot that gun; before you ended up in prison; and before death was at your door in the ghetto slums. Black leaders paved a way that was destructive. Sometimes we must look at all challenges we face, not just from the magician (system), but also our own people, because they were at the table creating things that weren't in the best interest of our people. They wanted education instead of showing our people how to build wealth and set up a business that would ultimately lead to business opportunities down the line. We can't see wealth because real wealth hasn't been seen by us. We have been led to go to school get an education; go in debt; go work for a living just to pay that loan back and invest in a 401(k) that will never materialize into nothing. Why is it so hard for Blacks to save money? One reason is because we never had extra cash, living paycheck to paycheck it' s hard to save, plus we love spending money before we even get it, by not having anything we are quick to spend, and "not having" also means knowledge about finances, not just material things. Instead of working a 9 to 5 and never making it out of poverty, create opportunity; make the table you sit at. Learn to create wealth and grow income, so multiple generations can succeed. Go to school, work, pay off debt, sleep and wake up and do it again. We were never taught the significance of ownership and entrepreneurship.

Our black leaders have also played a role in mass incarceration, not just the magician. Blacks have played a major role in criminal justice policies that bought about the tough-on-crime measures. Black voters, citizens, mayors, legislators, and prosecutors have had active roles in the shaping of reforms that led to mass incarceration. Since we were removed from slave ships, these blacks existed; two- timers. When crime was running through our communities, because of the heroin epidemic of the 60's and again in the 70's with crack, many black leaders pushed for harsher sentences, which in tum led to majority black cities and counties to incarcerate many of its own people. Even black leaders like Maxine Waters, led efforts to increase the maximum penalties for manufacturing PCP in the 1970's. Just as the federal and state governments did with crack and cocaine, where with crack a black defendant gets more time even though cocaine is still being used to manufacture crack. The real reason was because blacks used crack more than whites, and whites used raw cocaine over crack, black defendants got more time. Just like Mrs. Waters did for PCP in California in 1978, increased the time because of the manufacturing process of PCP; and who was doing the selling of PCP back then? Black drug dealers! They soon saw after years of the rise in incarceration, that increasing sentences didn't stop the sale of PCP, in fact in 1970's and 1980's, California, Maryland and other black communities saw an increase in the selling of PCP. Just as the crack led to low-level drug offenses being linked in the chain for mass incarceration, the PCP legislation in California led to South Central residents being sent to prison longer than whites. Even

Johnny Cochran, great lawyer, also played a part in handing down these harsh sentences to a district attorney. Mandatory minimum sentences were the norm and Blacks played a role in the development of them.

At this time between 1970 and 1980, crime was a problem because of drugs that were placed there by the (magician), also an even more troubling an economic war was going on, urban America was thinking because of factory jobs, but corporations moved these businesses overseas, that had a toll on black advancement and drove many into poverty in these communities. Once the factories left, the redlining began and thriving communities with home ownership were torn away and ghettos emerged. Houses were torn down, and Projects was built, Section 8 developed, and welfare formed. So, the focus shifted to the so-called "war on drugs", one of the most expensive and ineffective ways that the U.S. Government was fighting drug selling. While the war on drugs was happening, behind the curtain the magician was sending drugs into black communities, using puppets like Freeway Rick Ross to sell the drugs across the West Coast and Mid-West. These actions caused poverty to increase, mass incarceration to exist and unheard-of Black on Black murders to happen across this country. All the while the magician was allowing you to see an illusion, and we fed into this by selling drugs, killing each and building drug empires that lasted for short terms, until the F.B.I. comes and take everything away and claim as their own.

Out of these troubling times and out of poverty we built perseverance and the resilience that in turn allowed our people to survive. That hunger to succeed, to seek and create opportunity and see pass the traps the magician has placed before US, has allowed dour people to endure and still be here to again try and break out of this caste system, and poverty-stricken neighborhoods. Being poor allowed hunger to exist, now let's what should drive us.

[D]: Drive to Success

Being able to use those conditions as a driven force to succeed is a whole other thing and requires more than knowledge or knowing about a certain thing or two. Knowledge requires action to activate it and use it as a positive force to change your life. The odds are against us but were not ordinary people. 140 million people in this country are poor (43.5% of the population). 37 million without healthcare; 66 million works for less than 15 dollars an hour. Odds are odds, that don't mean that they can't be beaten. A plan, with knowledge, and action can beat the odds and tear down the illusion that has been placed before us. Rapper Killer Mike said it best: "where poverty ends, prosperity begins, and crime just starts to fade away." We can have plans that solve economic problems, debt, growing businesses, and investment strategies, but without action plans and knowledge is just information.

Ownership is everything; we don't own the stores in our communities. We have sold our hair care industry to Asians. The black dollar leaves the black community as soon as we purchase things from stores in our communities because we don't own anything. You can't generate wealth to put back into our communities if we don't own anything in our communities. So how do we get ownership? The usual way is to obtain capital from a bank, but access to this means of capital has been denied throughout history. No credit, no loan! Blacks have been denied loans because of no credit history. But how do you build credit in poverty? We create what doesn't exist to help our people; successful blacks need to help in this effort. I hate it when rich black leaders of business go on T.V. and say: "Well blacks have been denied access to money, resources, etc." None has ever said: I will create the capital by way of starting small banks in the communities, so we could stop getting denied! Stop searching for help and create opportunity, pool money, resources, and business ideas together. We have the likes of Jay-Z, Robert Smith, Oprah, Magic Johnson, Michael Jordan & David Steward. Many of them have talked about these social economic problems. Tyler Perry for instance, Tyler Perry was getting shot down by Hollywood for years, so he did it himself and created his own Hollywood in Atlanta, where his studio now sits and where he is the sole owner of it. Hollywood neglected Black actors for decades, wasn't producing any content from blacks like Tyler Perry's *Madea*. Seeing this disadvantage Perry built his own studio, which now allows him to produce whatever and give opportunities to others of his hue. Oprah always gets on T.V. and talk about how blacks and women of color especially can' t get opportunities, investments, and projects off the ground. So, Oprah why don't you create and invest? Start an investment bank with $100 million dollars to allow communities to have access to capital to start a business. (BANK BLACK) All these black Visionaries and Leaders of Business need to get together and form a plan (economic) to help people in poverty. We have sent people into space, invented multi-billion-dollar companies, but you mean to tell me that we can't solve the poverty problem that affects 43.5% or 140 million people in our country and multiple billion around the world? We can't because we are scared to try.

We as Blacks and people that come from poverty can look at the 1% and hate them or look at them and learn from their mistakes and success. The power of the black dollar is $1.1 Trillion dollars of those 2 cents of every dollar to Black business. Yes, the magicians have blocked us at every step from getting capital. We have too many successful blacks in this country to sit idle while poverty continues to hurt our community. Crate banks, VC's, grocery stores, comer stores, food stores, develop the supply chain that connects all communities in these improvised neighborhoods.

"Economic Agenda #1 Create Opportunity"

Credit companies will never consider things like rent payments, phone bill payments, or other forms of payments and bills people in poverty use. So, we create; instead of waiting to get credit building systems from big companies, we should be creating systems like one I developed around community-based banking, that's decentralized and uses artificial intelligence to readily see and read data and offer solution in seconds. Credit scores are based on phone data, bills, rent payments, and the community score of your fellow residents. Based on that, credit will be given out, loans will be processed in seconds and capital for future businesses will be sent to the account in minutes. Our future depends on ideas that enrich our fellow citizens. As you look at this from your prison cell, we always think that we can' t accomplish building credit from prison or we can't make sound investments from your cell. Don't be the "Negative Nanny" that sit in the rec. hall and tell you that "you are lying" or "you can't do that; the prison won't let you." This environment is not a positive place in the world, lost souls, mental health, and killers walk these halls. Remember, create opportunity is a slogan of the Pro Se Prisoner. Make your cell your office, write your plan, and act on it. Credit can be built from prison, so here is your chance.

www.creditstrong.com

This website allows you to build credit from prison on a monthly payment plan; no money is given to you upfront, once the payment covers the loan the money is released. For example, take a look at the previous "Hungry" section to see details of the plan. But that was an opportunity to create, and they did. Being as though most people fail to pay their credit cards off, credit strong took the money off the table at the initial stage gave an incentive of 120 transaction once paid, and developed a $15, $50, or $100 a month plan that would allow most low-income people to get involved.

Poverty is a learned created condition that affects 140 million people in the U.S. So why hasn't the richest, most advanced country in the world solved this problem? Think! Why has poverty not been solved? My opinion is that, keeping people living paycheck-to-paycheck, under the $15 dollar a hour threshold, keeps them depending on the rich company that employs them. The rich controls 80-90% of the wealth generated, people in poverty are the workforce it needs to maintain their wealth. Look at all the companies that have fought the $45 min. wage laws. The cost of living has risen in the past 25-30 years. But paychecks and the min. wage have stayed the same. The solution creates opportunity and builds a company or business and invests in your community, which will allow you to help the next person out of poverty.

Sitting in your cell you must utilize your time to shape your ideas and create. What are your solutions to solve the poverty problem? Start thinking about ways to create wealth, stop trying to become rich. Wealth is created by owning assets that appreciate in value. Also, investing and saving plays a role in wealth creation. The rich use investment strategies like "compounding". "Asset Allocation", divide your assets across different classes, or investments. One way to look at saving is: when you get a money order set aside a portion of the money that you will put aside $10 a month, $20 a month, or $25 a month. Also, you can do it with prison jobs, small steps to train yourself to build savings to create opportunities in the future to buy assets that appreciate in value. There is money in this country and wealth that's up for grabs. What will you create to partake? The world is changing around us, in 2020 viruses like COVID-19 kills whoever and whatever, tech is changing. If we don't take part in this future technology, we will fall off a cliff and never recover.

"Economic Agenda #2
Home Ownership"

Laws were passed that prohibited black from buying homes in the suburbs around the 20th Century. Redlining and other measures stopped blacks from gaining ground. Although the Fair Housing Act (1968) helped somewhat and Fannie Mae allowed changes to some rules, that allow lenders to consider nontraditional credit data from black citizens, there are still problems and access to capital from banks that are not in the neighborhood are a major problem. Block grants exist, alone with FITA loans, VA loans and USDA loans for rural borrowers. Good people around the country help people, start foundations, give money to support a cause or action, and finance businesses of minorities. Every year, instead of going out of business because the need is gone and people move out of poverty with their help, they start over helping a new list of poverty-stricken people. Ask yourself: why haven't these foundations solved the problem? If this was a business, and every year you lose money without return on capital or growth, that business with tank! So, if each year we have foundations that feed the poor, house the poor, give money to the poor, only to turn around and give the same resources to new people who are poor each year, how is that helping or fixing a problem?

Agreed we should help the poor, but we should create opportunities to get secure a future for them. There is saying: "Why give a man a fish, when you can teach him how to fish." After he learns how to fish; he teaches the next person from his community and next thing you know fish markets open to sell the fish, people buy fish in the community that money stays in the community to finance other ventures, next thing you know fishing stores open to buy equipment and then a Boat Business springs up, totally off of that foundation teaching rather than supply a meal for one day.

History has a way of answering problems. So, let's look at history to see what blacks the last time did, the magician blocked housing, loans, and shopping in their stores. Great blacks stepped up to answer the call to the pressing issues of economics that they weren't included in. Harriet Tubman wanted to free slaves, so she created the Underground Railroad to free them. Other people created rising cities from the ground up: San Francisco, CA; Eden, Florida; Kansas; Tulsa, Oklahoma, and the most successful at that time were Hayti, Durham, North Carolina. In North Carolina, we were prohibited from shopping in their stores, banking in their banks and getting insurance, even though they were insuring horses and not humans. So great leaders came together to succeed, they created opportunity; blocked from insurance, the people saw opportunity to create, one of the most successful business in N.C.: (NC Mutual Life Insurance). Banks wouldn't lend money to start a business or fund other opportunities, (Mechanics and Farmers Banks) were built that funded business ventures throughout the city. So, to build wealth in a poverty-stricken place, the citizens kept the black dollar rotating in their community (! 00% of it). Today only 2 cents of every dollar spent stays in our neighborhoods. Even worse, in 2020 that's only for about 6 hours that it stays there. By building wealth community by community and owning the businesses in the community, this allowed for wealth to be generated and for each community citizens to take part in obtaining financial freedom.

"When told no? Then create what you ask for"

-C.A. Knuckles

In Wilmington, NC the same strategy was being taken up. Around 1890 Wilmington was North Carolinas biggest city. To build wealth, they pooled money together to build two (2) small banks that loaned money to community members starting businesses. Law firms, Doctor's offices were built and help generate income in the community. At that time the richest Blackman in Wilmington was Thomas C. Miller, an auctioneer who built an empire around real estate. When we were given an opportunity after slavery, we thrived· and the magician didn't like that all these "Black Wall Street's" were being built around the country. White Supremacy groups, burned, blew-up and killed thousands of blacks in almost every town that had black wealth. From Tulsa to Wilmington, then the Federal Government got involved and broke up black wealth by building the National Interstate Highway right through these rich black communities, at a time some called "Urban Removal". This was a planned attack by the Federal Government to break-up these successful towns. Then came the Housing Act in the 1950s-1960s, that forced thousands of blacks from their homes. These communities' lost poverty rights and land rights. Housed was torn down to make way for Housing Projects, that led to poverty-stricken ghettos, that we have not recovered from yet.

Things are different today; there is more black wealth in this country than at any time in our history. Black billionaires thrive as do multi-millionaires. But while these things have occurred these same black billionaires as Oprah, and the millionaires in the black universe talk on T.V. about these problems, and all these struggles of common folk but none has even come close to helping the effort to create like our black leaders of yesterday. Community based banking, building grocery stores, insurance companies, personal service businesses, etc. WHY HAVEN'T THE BLACK ELITE DONE THIS? That's hard to answer, only they can answer that, but the media doesn't ask these questions of those people. If we can't create, then stop complaining!

Being in prison I have time to sit for 14 hours a day and plan and research the root causes of prison and poverty. Most people don't even know about these business leaders after slavery, they know about slavery and then jump to Jim Crow and Mass Incarceration. There was a period between slavery ending and Jim Crow that was of great importance, to us, from the financial and educational standpoint. You're in prison, thinking how to get out, but the only way to stay out is to know how you got there-not when you were convicted or took the plea-but when your neighborhood turned into an economic wasteland and poverty-stricken high crime ghetto. Also, learning how not to ask for permission and create opportunity is also important. Staying out of prison also comes with knowing about financial literacy, this will help secure your future. If you want to be working for the rich, then put this book down and fill out a job application upon release and continue to struggle. If you want to create your future and build wealth, then this book is for you.

Driven to success is the last part of a journey in which you seek financial knowledge and act upon it. You must realize that the magician has placed destruction in front of you to distract you from what's out there, hoping to kill your Drive to succeed, and stunt your educational goals. What the magician banks on is that you will give up and stay blinded by his illusion. But as history has shown our forefathers and fore mothers always fought for better days and no matter if we were born into poor ghettos, that hunger and drive was built into us and passed down from slavery to the 21st century. Now tapping into it is what separates us apart. Knowledge about these conditions and how to create rather than complain will help us out. Remember, prison is just a symptom of drugs, racial issues and redlining black communities. My goal is to give the knowledge so you can act on that knowledge and create opportunity. Despite being locked-up, intelligent men/women are behind these walls, searching for chances to showcase their potential. No excuses will be given about the actions that got them here, only ideas on how to gain freedom, financial wealth, and self-help while behind bars that will assist them, and other prisoners once released and behind bars for prisoners who will never be released. Instead of hating prisoners who you haven't taken the time to understand, try understanding first before you pass judgment that will affect that person' s life. Listen to our stories before you decide to throw away the key, let us show you our potential while inside; our growth we have accomplished and our future plans of creating opportunity for us and our community.

The magician suspects you to play the game, with deadly consequences of death or prison which have you really thinking that it's your only option. The streets give young black men and women growing up false power. If that power only works in your city or neighborhood with drug dealers like you, then that's not power. If it doesn't affect or force change that's not power.

Change is hard in any circumstance, even harder when it comes to changing the mind of someone who grew up in ghetto. Those who thinks selling drugs in the community to your own people is the best way to make it out of poverty and improvised neighborhoods. The government creates these ghettos and bears responsibility for the destruction there racial, and economic oppression caused, but it's our responsibility to create our own opportunity to fix our communities. We are not even engaging in real financial wealth creation in these ghettos, we are selling drugs until the police come take it away. We are also eradicating each other to a point where our communities are more dangerous than actual war zones. The drive to success is in us, past down from our slave ancestors who created it to fight the ills of slavery, Jim Crow, colored codes, and the lynching of our people. We then took that drive and applied the wrong way, to a wrong deadly cause, because that's what the magician showed you were the only way to be financially independent. (Dealing drugs)

Our knowledge of wealth or lack thereof has been formed, not by looking past the comer, but by standing on the comer. Real knowledge can only come from experience.

"All genuine knowledge originates in Direct experience"

-Mao Zedong

All our experiences have been negative ones that have harmed us at every step. This book is to give you the experience to read and learn your positive history so we can grasp our greatness in the financial world. It's hard to get information in prison, I can't count how many phone calls I've made to get this information. To be a true Prose Prisoner you must block the noise of your tier or cell block, study every day, create opportunity, and be able to rehabilitate yourself. You're sent to prison for punishment for a crime, not rehabilitation. The magician's goal is that you come to prison and leave worse off than when you came. That will get you back in prison (Recidivism) and destroy your community even more once you return to it. We have seen and learned of the problem we face financial from behind bars. So, what's your solution? What's your plan? How will you create opportunity?

Look around the prison and you will see entrepreneurs conducting business. Coffee, food bags, drawing pictures, legal work, tier stores, sewing clothes, and making baked goods for sale. But if you are released you lose this drive to succeed. We go back to what we know: Selling drugs, because it's easy to accomplish, and easy to obtain; doesn't require much effort to sell. Also, most jobs won' t hire a convicted felon. You are thinking small, think big! Be a Prose Prisoner and use that drive to succeed in business, the problem is you lack the knowledge to succeed, and while you were in prison you sold coffee shots for profit, but you didn't sit and learn financial knowledge and literacy for the real world. That plan you never developed in prison, the one in your head you thought you would remember without writing it down. Developing that business plan allows you to leave prison and go right into legit business owner. I will help you develop that plan and show some legit business that costs from a couple hundred dollars to a thousand dollars. Applying this acquired knowledge to your plan will allow you to be a successful Prose Prisoner, because you will have done it on your own. Once you open the door, help someone else get out of misery and create opportunities that allow them to secure their future. How successful you want to be is up to you, I just let you know your history, and some ways to start your successful business. THE ACTION YOU TAKE IS UP TO YOU, NOT ME.

"We're all born ignorant, but one must Work hard to remain stupid"

-Benjamin Franklin

"Organized knowledge that is put to use is power"

-Napoleon Hill

Great minds ask great questions, and you should always proceed with these thoughts. Ask yourself why? Why are these conditions so harsh? How did our communities become so poor, crime ridden, and economically depressed? What you seek answers for, also ask yourself to question that challenge what you have done to better things. Have I tried to create opportunities where there were none? If not, why? Thinking big will allow you to see past the prison cell and see your future being secured. Prose Prisoners think big and conquer great obstacles.

Up until your "knowledge moment", your life has been wasted, due to you not being able to see past the magician efforts to step your growth and to quell your drive to success. We like to think we have been controlling our lives; we sit in prison cells saying I "control" my life, but it's an illusion. Your ancestors never wanted future generations to go through Jim Crow, Colored Codes, and Mass Incarceration. This story was written before you were born, you grew up under the magician's illusion without even knowing it. Your community didn't give you answers or knowledge on how to escape, but you had a suspicion that things were not right, but again you sold drugs, robbed, killed, and destroyed your community because you never thought anything else was possible. Always ask why? This quest to success and knowledge was always in you, it just needs water *action* to feed the plant *brain* so it can grow *self*. Without those three things above you will become stagnant and die. Pro Se Prisoners do things themselves and grow as a result. Now you have your Ph.D. Poor, Hungry and Driven to Success well sort of, there's still one last test for you to accomplish: Putting all you have learned into action. So, let's move to the next chapter, and test your Drive to Success.

"The difference between rich people and poor people is where they sign their checks. Poor people sign the front. Rich people sign the back"

-Ric Edelman

Utilizing Your Ph.D.

How will you be an asset to your community? Answer this question with honesty now that you know, there are no more excuses. You must now move throughout your prison and share your wisdom on the unknowledgeable amongst you. Go there of your own free will, to teach the truth to those who are being left behind and still under the magicians' illusions.

"Knowledge is the pathway from slavery to freedom"

-Frederick Douglass

Your current conditions were planned; Black poverty planned as well. The magician set up the conditions and obstacles by way of the "sleight of hand trick". Then sit on the sideline and talk about us badly to their cohorts.

"To see the outside world read and obtained knowledge that's how I escaped the chains locked around my brain."

-C.A. Knuckles

There will always be barriers that keep poor people out of the business world but using what you know now you are ahead of the curb. I look at prisoners and smile because where can you give knowledge to unlimited untapped brain power that will help them secure their future.

The Knowledge Plan

The first plan should be the knowledge plan. This seems obvious; must discover self before being able to teach someone else or put action into your own plans. Without knowing it you have already done that by getting this book. Securing your financial future while behind bars requires hard work. Odds won't be in your favor at first, but once you read the knowledge you will be on your way. Knowledge by itself is just information, with any information you must try to comprehend it, and apply it. I told you the problems and the solution, so it's up to you to come up with your own "Economic Agenda: Create Opportunity" for your community. The Knowledge Questions:

-What is knowledge? Why do I need it?

-What books will I order?

-Why should I change my ways?

-Is change like this possible?

-How will gaining knowledge help me?

-How will I turn mistakes into opportunities?

Before reading this your knowledge didn't let you understand the magician's process. Your brain only knew drugs and as a result death or prison will come along. But what you don't realize is that you were born in the magicians' game of abject poverty with a curtain in front of that blocked your view, which didn't allow you to see your potential, or uncover your Ph.D. that was in your subconscious mind waiting to be activated. Only light can get you out of a darkroom. Just as knowledge can only get you out of poverty and secure your financial future. Not knowing keeps you relying on the rich for guidance; knowing allows you to help the community get out of poverty and decide on your own path in life. Your knowledge plan must be thought out and expressed out loud to attract those things in life. This plan should be used to rewrite your story, from abject poverty to successful businessman or women. Your whole life up until this point was based on negative energy, "so you think, so you become," your brain only was wired for death or prison, and that's what you got. Once again, you're at a crossroad in your life you left the streets (negative) to emerge in prison (negative) but unlike the streets while in prison you wrote how you will get the knowledge you need to change your mind set.

Write down how you thought before reading this book and how you thought after you read it. Put it in your knowledge plan. Compare the streets and prison life, and lastly describe your journey with dates and details of your life and how it changed once you were knowledgeable. I used to always think of getting out of prison and getting rich. The only problem was I had no plan to do so, or no ideas but selling drugs. I was a kid in prison, got sentenced to 15 years old, and with no sense of what was coming once I entered adult prison. I blamed others for my mistakes and my first 2 years in prison was crazy; running around like I know better than anybody; getting in trouble until I ran into a cell wall and couldn't go anywhere. That cell wall was administrative segregation for 3 years. At that point I vowed to change, and I did, I wrote my plan out and stuck to it, so almost 16 years later I successfully completed all but two things on my knowledge plan, and that's: Become a billionaire, and start a nonprofit legal foundation to help other obtain their freedom. My knowledge plan started with non-fiction business books, and about poverty in my community. Your start might be something else. What do you know now about yourself? Why do you think you lacked knowledge? Once you know the destructive power of the magician, then you will excel at all costs to break down the illusion that poverty, crime, and drug dealing is all you can do, with death or prison as the end result. Your knowledge plan will allow you to become a Prose Prisoner fully aware of your potential to create opportunity and not complain but take action to create.

The Freedom Plan

It goes without saying that you must also write out how you will obtain your freedom. This is important because getting home is a top priority in the Grand plan which includes (3) plans. As a - successful Jailhouse Lawyer in Maryland, this plan is dearest to my heart, because every case I complete is a story of great despair, importance, and challenge. The criminal justice system destroys lives with reckless abandonment, and with no care of the story behind the crime. As you know Public Defenders Offices around this country are underfunded and understaffed to meet the needs of the community it was created to serve. So, this Freedom Plan must take that into consideration when writing out your plan. Write out all the legal avenues you have (i.e.- Direct Appeal) and so forth. Make yourself well informed of every step in the process so you can plan around that, and you don't waive issues because of deadlines. Also, how much lawyers in this field charge? What lawyer do you think gives you the best way forward? Your plan should speak to legal process, finances for lawyers, and who do you need to write to help with things. Judge name and address should be in there, so you always have. When this is written out you can already have your next move planned out. Just remember that your incarceration was planned by the magician (system) before you had any say in the matter. Learn from his illusions and never fall victim again. Also, check out FreebirdPublishers.com for legal books that help.

The Money Plan

You will need to utilize your Ph.D. in full to design this plan. Developing your ideas starts with what your passion is. Also, as the Ph.D. shows, you must really become a social entrepreneur to solve community problems. Social Entrepreneurship is taking a business approach to effectively solving a social problem. The Ph.D. approach is more than just making money for yourself but developing an economic agenda that helps the next man or woman make money and create opportunity in your improvised neighborhood.

"Change your mental state, so that You will feel confident"

-Tony Robbins

Prison officials don't want you to change, if they did there, would be rehabilitation efforts going on in prison, rather than idle time filled with drugs and killings. You were kept in cells to stop your thinking, so you must use it to expand it. What you don't understand, you should confront, and that's what this money plan is all about. Create financial knowledge by confronting the fact that you don't know anything about it. Your idea should be geared towards where the opportunity lies. Or where your passion is at, your passion can create opportunity in other people's lives. Something that's of high value to someone else has potential to succeed.

Idea to Opportunity

- Opportunity can be found or made.

- Research and capture of ideas is called: Opportunity recognition.

- You must feel, check, plan, and act.

- If you need help with an idea, there are websites that can help: halfbakery.com, coolbusinessideas.com, and ideaswatch.com

- One trait you must have been creativity: A process producing an idea or opportunity that is novel and useful frequently derived from making connections among distinct ideas or opportunities.

- Having an imagination that thinks big and beyond these prison walls is key.

-

"Imagination is more important than knowledge. Knowledge is limited"

- Albert Einstein.

- Your imagination will give you your ideas, but you must decide whether it's an opportunity for you or just another failure.

- You must write down all your ideas, so you don't forget them. One good idea can give you the opportunity to succeed.

- Look at problems and come up with a solution. Remember poverty has set you on the path of success. What are some problems with the ghettos and rural areas around the country? Banking, credit, housing policies is bad, welfare, crime, drugs, and low-paying jobs. What can be designed, created, or used to help solve this problem while also benefiting from those ideas?

- What separates you from your fellow prisoners? Can you draw, run a store on the tier, or sell food bags? Take that idea and expand it to the outside world by thinking big.

- Also remember that owning your own business is "key" to being a Prose Prisoner. Having a small business gives opportunity to you. For instance, people living in poverty have needs most wealthy people don't have. There are places in rural and urban America without a grocery store or a local place to buy prescription (pharmacy).

- When developing an idea, if it doesn't work out the first time try again. You will develop perseverance that will help you achieve your goal. It never hurts to ask for help if you need it. Just learn from your failures and pivot if you must.

- Your idea to create opportunity will and can have multiple streams of income for you. Produce a product, invest in stocks and real estate, or solve a problem that exists.

Your method should not be limited to one idea or concept, broaden your search.

- Always remember no business can endure unless it fills a need. The best ideas can be found in poverty, because they lack the bask things that the middle class and upper class has. From plumbing to banking. Urban and rural areas are "banking deserts", with massive financial upside. Look at the news and you will see the ghetto streets filled will junk/trash stacked high as gates. The first car was invented because of the massive amount of "shit", from horses that was pilling up in the neighborhoods and alleys back in the day, so some creative people thought of a better way to solve two (2) problems: horse shit and the lack of sustainable transportation. So, you must look at the trash/junk then piling up as an idea to create opportunity. Creating a "Junk Removal" Service will allow you to get a city, county, or state contract and for your neighborhood up at the same time. At Prose Prisoner Way!

- Keep in mind that it's 2020. and people want mobile on demand things, they also want it fast like Amazon Prime. The future is mobile; you can reach more people and gain the biggest market share of the pie.

- If you just want to make money then you can't be a Prose Prisoner, we provide something that solves a real problem, whole create opportunity for the community by which we come from.

Whatever the idea, make sure your dedicated, write it down, develop and write a plan, and secure your financial future by way of creating opportunities.

Opportunity to Business

This business plan serves as a planning tool for growth, a plan that shows potential investors information viable to evaluate the company, and a base to measure performance overtime. Without one you just have an idea, not a functioning business. (Start-up)

Business Plan Format

Cover Page: Contain contact information.

Table of Contents: Quick guide to information.

Executive Summary: Explains business prospect.

Company Description: Historical account of company.

The Product of Service: What's unique about service?

The Market: Create a picture of the market where your business competes.

Marketing: Informs your readers of how you plan to sell and promote your business.

Management/Ownership: Introduces the leadership of the business.

Competition: Completion's strengths and weaknesses.

Financial Statements and Projections: Blank sheet, income statement, cash flow statementand financial forecasts.

Appendices: Contains resumes of leadership,' positions and responsibilities of that leadership. Also, contains market data to back up claims of the whole business plan.

Don't look at this as too hard, because a lot of these things won't apply to just starting out, so as you begin to sell your service and/or product, go back to the business plan and rewrite the parts you couldn't fill-in pre-income. Practice makes perfect. Failures are vehicles to learn from.

Business Plan to Forming Company

This process will test your patience at first. What structure to use to form your company comes down to what's in your best interest? Some include:

Sole proprietorship: You are the one owner. You use a "fictitious name certificate" at your local state government office. If you choose to not use your name as the (sole proprietorship) this certificate will tell people you're the owner. It's really a (D.B.A.) "Doing Business As", write to your local state government (State's Secretary of State) or (State Taxation Office) to obtain one.

Key Points

- Complicated to sell business assets.

- Existence if you die, then the business dies.

- May need business licenses, sales tax license, or permits.

- You have personal liability for all debt and obligations.

- You and your business are taxed as one for income purposes.

Limited Liability Company (LLC)

- Requires Articles of Organization which will have to be filed with the Secretary of Stata.

- Members must enter into an Operating Agreement.

- The (LLCs) limit liability for its members and taxes pass through.

- The number of investors is unlimited and can have foreign members.

Key Points

- Members not liable for debts.

- Management operates under an agreement.

- Free to decide how profit and losses are split up.

- Upon formation, you must follow state law.

- Can choose how taxed. Pass through/taxed as a separate entity.

- Operating Agreement controls the right to transfer of member's interests.

You are in prison; these are the two best options for starting a business. The benefits of this way of conducting your business are so important because it allows you to benefit from taxes (lower) and protects your assets when people get lawsuit happy. Understanding the 1% business habits is key to your success. All the 1% businesses are first started in two (2) states: Nevada and Delaware. The reason: NO STATE INCOME TAXES! That means more money in your pocket and lower tax bills or even none at all. Look at Apple, in the U.S.A. and Europe, they weren't pay taxes for years, because their lawyers did what they were paid to do: find tax havens, and tax loopholes for the company. This saved them billions of dollars and made the lawyers millions. Learn from them, you want the best, you must pay for it, or if you're good with numbers learn the TAX CODE! You can obtain proper tax forms from the I.R.S. website (irs.gov) they also have booklets and packets that explain the proper way to file taxes. Also, obtain a copy of the latest tax rates and tax code for your review.

"D.B.A." Doing Business As

In Maryland this is the way the D.B.A looks. Before doing anything, file a D.B.A to ensure you protect your name and to see if anybody has that name. This will also allow you to easily act and start-up your "sole proprietorship" from prison. It's just a fill in the blank form as shown below.

Financial Power of Attorney

Because of the setting up of business bank accounts and personal bank.- accounts, you will need someone you trust to set-up these for you. There are companies that do this kind of work, but most have scammed prisoners out of money. Also, set out a list of financial jobs or tasks that must be completed, along with the Power of Attorney Contract. Below is a general multi-page financial Power of Attorney Contract.

The Money Plan is steps to financial success, you don't need security, and you're in prison with the best security known to man. Take the steps to protect what's yours, don't ever forget that! People take notice of brands everybody wants: Prada, Gucci, Polo, Red bottoms, Coogi and Roll Royce's. These companies were built as a branded brand; name recognition, and constantly being- talked about by the consumer. My brand is: Prose Prisoner. Whatever you decide on is your own thing. Stand out from everybody else and protect your brand at all costs. You must do the following to protect your brand:

1) Use godaddy.com to claim your name as a website. This costs from $9-$20 depending on the name. The best names are ones that's created by the owner: IBM; Microsoft. Buy the domain name for your brand/or business. (e.g., www.proseprisoner.com) that's mine.

2) Claim brand on (Yelp.com and Wikipedia)

3) Email: obtain e-mail account from G-mail, to have an e-mail associated with your brand. (e.g.:

www.proseprisoner@gmail.com) Yours should look like the above address once completed.

Another area of protection is copyright and trade marking your idea, name, logo, etc.

Copyright

Copyrighting is when you protect written work, such as songs, books, paintings, photographs, movies, and other works expressed in physical form. Companies can also copyright video material and their books/reports. To apply to copyright your work contact:

Library of Congress
U.S. Copyright Office Publications Section
101 Independence Avenue, SE #6304
Washington, DC 20559-6304

Ask them to send you (Form CO), so you can apply for a copyright for your work. Or online at www.copyright.gov

Trademark

A trademark is a word, phrase, symbol or design, or a combination of them. Your business or brand name is an example, along with the logo, slogan, and symbol. You must apply for an application from the below address or online at: www.uspto.gov.

U.S. Patent and Trademark
600 Dulany Street
Alexandria, VA 22314

Remember always protecting, so you have legal authority to determine how your brand name, logo, and books will be used in future business dealings. The Prose Prisoner way is about do-it-yourself, while at the same time creating opportunity for your fellow prisoners and community. Take small steps, it's a lot to go over in this book and my next one after this, but study, learn the history and always protect the brand and think big!

Unique Ways to Make Money

After you have protected your brand, now let's get into the money. Starting small means finding a couple ways to get a couple dollars in your pocket, while in prison or once released, remember this is still "Your Money Plan", don't forget about that, something is better than nothing.

Knowing and understanding basic accounting budgeting, and growing a business is key, no matter if you're starting out small or big. These concepts may be hard for the average prisoner living off a state pay, but with proper financial knowledge you can turn that state pay into a money machine, just by using the above (3) three concepts to their advantage. Wealth creation starts with these three concepts; stop thinking about today and focus on building multi-generation wealth.

From prison you can become a writer like me. There are multiple ways to write from prison such as books, eBooks, newspaper, online news website and blogging. What do you offer? Do you have expertise in a field? Do you like to write short stories? The thing about writing is that you must have a passion for it because it will show in your work. In prison prisoners always need things typed up if you invest in a $300 typewriter you can become the go to guy for legal typing or book typing for the population. Find the jailhouse lawyer and offer your services to him/her for a fee. Write out a contract, that spells out specifically what you will do and how much you will get paid. You may not be a writer, so use your new type- writer to get paid off the writers. You can charge prisoners (per word). Remember one page can contain up to 400 words. Or charge (per page), but in prison it's more feasible to charge (per-project). A legal petition can run $50, a book can run $5 for every (20 pages). So, it's up to you, so whether you write or type it's a lucrative business either way. Treat it like a business and don't pay yourself until expenses are paid. (Ribbons, corrections tap, paper, etc.)

Getting Outside Clients: You can start by sending general query letters to prison base magazines, newsletters, and other prison publications, seeking info. on potential jobs or offer yourself as a writer of legal, fiction, or news stories. Whatever you're knowledgeable about. Be persuasive in your query letter and offer up some examples of your writings. For example, Prison Legal News pays prisoners for writing, so if you know the law and could help people out then you should send a query letter there. A good book to get on this subject is "Write and Get Paid", from Amazon/or freebirdpublishers.com

Drawing: Besides writing, another proven method is drawing. I know prisoners who make $200-$300 for one picture of prisoners loved ones. Easily by setting up an LG. page, Facebook, and e mail account, you can offer your talents to the outside world for a major cash payday. Citizens on the outside pay a lot of money for Graphic Designers that do logos, websites, and develop art galleries. You have a unique advantage being in prison because if guys in prison will pay $200-$300 for artwork, most people in society will pay 2x that for many different designs. You also can set-up and sell your artwork on websites like: Etsy.com; Squarespace.com; and Pinterest.com

Writing: When deciding whether to write a book from prison, setting yourself up for success is important. Many may struggle to write; set-up plans and goals of when and how many pages you will do a day. Find a topic, or idea you think the world would love to hear and write about it.

Also, if you have an idea for a book but writing isn't your thing then you could outsource your writing. Using an outside writer is common in the writing world and helpful. There are skillful prisoners who will be happy to write your book for you if paid an okay sum. Form a partnership type business contract between the two of you. Offer some money or a (%) percentage of the book sales.

It's your choice, so choose wisely whatever the decision. Some resources to also work into can be found in the "Resources" section in the back of the book.

"The richest people in the world look for and build networks; everyone else looks for networks". -Robert T. Kiyosaki

"Rich Dad, Poor Dad

Business with Minimum Investments

As a Pro se Prisoner, you must go about things on your own. That's the

concept: "oneself '. Because of this, we can spot investments with little or no money own. Out of that we create opportunities for others. Here are a few businesses that are available to start with low overhead. Learn from the 1%ers and own everything!

U-Haul Dealer

www.uhaul.com/dealer Start-up costs: $500-$1000

U-Haul University provides classes online that will assist in your transition. You will be able to make up to $75k to $150k by operating one of these dealerships. Scout out a location in a high traffic area, a sizable lot so trucks and trailers may be stored. Even in the ghetto, people will pay $19.95 to move items and often is the citizens who move the most. By placing it in these improvised neighborhoods, you can hire from those neighborhoods and provide an opportunity for the citizens that live there. Sky is the limit with this one.

Amazon Delivery Service Partner

Amazon allows you to operate your own package delivery business. You have autonomy to create your own company. Also, you can start your own logistics company, and partner with Amazon, thus having your own business. There will be a fleet of delivery vehicles to oversee; you hire and manage your own team. It's simple as visiting (logistics.amazon.com), to learn more about the amazing process. By partnering with Amazon, you will be able to hire and create opportunities for people while building wealth. If you have somebody on the outside you trust, then start the process with them as a partner and get them to manage the business as a partner with you, use your financial Power of Attorney representative to help your business partner with the application and forms. You can create a separate company and use that company to go into business with Amazon, that way you are established already. There aren't obstacles, but only opportunities, so think outside the box and get started creating opportunities. The cost is free if accepted.

Auto Rescue Service

Society has shifted to an "on-demand", "right-now" service. Mobile Apps and Amazon have allowed people to order a product or service and get it the same day or the next day. There is a need for Auto rescue service.

Here is an idea (TAKE IT!) Develop an App called: "ON-DEMAND AUTO", this service will allow anyone to download your app and geo-location will take over to tell you where they are or what service they require. This can include a tow, oil change, tire fix/change, dead battery, glass repair, locked keys in car, or needs a computer diagnostic problem. All this on-demand and within a couple minutes of reaching your destination. Think big like Amazon for Auto Services, Fast, reliable, and priced below coverage. Depending on a geographical area, you could charge anywhere from $50-$75 per service call. People will pay for "on-demand service" instead of driving to an auto-shop.

SET-UP: Register Business with a D.B.A., get liability insurance.

VEHICLE: You can get a tow truck, a mechanical truck, from any auction for a couple thousand dollars. To start get a pick-up truck, brand with logo, app name and number. Go to a discount Auto-store and buy the basic things like portable jumpstart cables, air compressor, portable lights, emergency flares and cones. You will need this at a bear-minimum, then once you make money you can gradually move up to tow trucks and full mechanic mode. To get the bare min. above, you

will have a cost of about: $800.00 dollars (not bad) This will include business registration and license, phone, credit card processing capability, Insurance, Business cards, tools above, Invoice Pad.

The building of the App should happen after you have started making money. Getting an Auto Service App will cost a couple thousand dollars, so research potential companies to do it for you, or some domain registers have that in their plans like (godaddy.com). When you build a website, you can also develop an app, so research and stack your money for this investment.

Cleaning Service

This is a flexible business that has a low-cost set-up cost. As a service operator you will be paid for cleaning homes, apartments, offices, and businesses. Just with any other business here, you must first register your D.B.A. name with your city or county. File for a Tax identification number from your state. Make sure to also check to see if your state requires a license for a cleaning business. Start off as a sole proprietorship, and then once a business picks up change it to an LLC. to get tax credits and protections. Buying a $200 dollar a year insurance policy is a good idea for this type of business. Also get bonding protection for theft, this will protect you and your client. For this type of business, you need to hit the ground running and develop relationships with Apartment Building Managers, Realtors, Rental Property Managers, and office building reps. Creating a marketing brochure, explaining services will help you get contract with these people. Make phone calls don't wait until they reach out. Create business cards with company logo, email, phone number, and address for about $600 dollars-including all the above-you can start your cleaning business. Cleaning supplies will be a monthly expense with you spending about $60 dollars a month on supplies. When using your own car, make sure you keep track of the mileage you use for business, so you can get a tax deduction for it.

Once you get established you can begin to create opportunities for someone else and start hiring a crew to execute multiple locations at a time, while you look for the next opportunity or contract.

Concierge Car Wash / Mobile Car Wash

Again, just like the Auto repair business think big on-demand. You can do the same for a car wash and detail business. Create an app and watch the money roll in obtaining buckets, sponges, whisk broom, and rags shouldn't break the bank. Set up business like I explained in the previous auto repair service section. Market your business at salons, hotels, restaurants, and anywhere people gather. Also, a business tip: you can have help, not as employees, but as contractors, so you can use form 1099 (irs.gov). About $700 dollars will get you up and running- this includes insurance, bonding, and equipment. Think big and tum old businesses over on their head, by using technology to bring it into the 21st century.

Some other businesses that will help you get off the ground are:

- Fitness/personal trainer

- Graphic Arts Designer

- Mobile Oil Change Service

- Personal Assistant

- Tile/Grout Specialist

- Virtual Assistant

- Writer

- Artist

Although not all the above may help or be in your wheelhouse, starting small will help you develop the skills for the great idea and wealth building system you develop. Write a plan; take action as a Prose Prisoner.

Fast Money

Quick ways to make money while in prison or outside of prison once released.

- Take part in Medical Trials

- Join Revenue Sharing Websites

- Sell Amazon Products by writing reviews

- Create an investment club and recommend stocks

- Freelance your Talent (www.elance;com)(odesk.com)

- Share your Opinion (start blog) (www.blogger.com)

- Write an e-book and sell it on Kindle

- Sell Art on Esty.com

- Parking Lot clean-up (www.cleanlots.com)

- Create a kickstarter.com project

These and many other are out there to start while in prison or upon release, these are to help you get started, my next book: Prose Prisoner: Alternative Investments (Guide to Wealth) will pick-up where this book leaves off and show you how to build wealth the I% way, by using tax loopholes, Corporations, Insurance and 1031 Real Estate exchanges. But you must crawl before you walk and these ideas will get your feet wet in the business field, learn from your mistakes, and know that you are well on your way to building wealth the Prose Prisoner way.

Business Checklist

As a felon the odds of finding a job are slim, so instead of filling out a job application, fill out an application to form an LLC. Build wealth; don't create wealth for the 1% by working all your life for an illusion of a 401(k) or social security (of which is going bankrupt). A website called **bonds4jobs.com** allows businesses to hire felony convicted citizens, with the backing of bonds to insure them for taking a chance. For the people who don't want to build wealth but work for someone else, this program is for you. Not every prisoner has that drive to succeed like others. Hopefully, you learned something by reading this book and I thank you.

Remember, you must have a website you can use (**godaddy.com**, **wix.com** (free), and **weebly.com**) (**justhost.com**) (has domain and hosting) next get business cards printed with all valuable information printed on them. (**www.overnightprints.com**) (**www.vistaprint.com**) or (**Office Depot and/or Kinko's**). Use pay-pal as a payment processing option for your online products or services. One good thing about using GoDaddy websites services is that it has built in e-commerce capability. Branding is everything, when coming up with a business name, make it unique. Check with your States Secretary of State to see if the name is available. See **"Resource"** section for website info. Register name if not taken with them, do the same name when buying domain registration for website.

Important! Check with your States Dept. of Revenue **for Sales Tax** info, and how to collect them. Also, while there get **State Tax Identification number** (free). Also, you must get a tax id number from (irs.gov) for free. They will also have a link for your state, to obtain the free tax id number.

I hope you planned ahead and take advantage of what credit strong.com has to offer to build credit while behind bars. Because getting a business checking account is key to your growth. But if you haven't been building your credit or have bad credit don't worry, I have a quick solution for you.

STEP 1: Get Wal-Mart Prepaid Debit Card (free if you deposit a minimalmonthly amount)

STEP 2: With that Wal-Mart Card open a free Pay-Pal Account.

STEP 3: Get the free Pay-Pal business debit card. Cashing checksat banks wherethey were written.

There is always a plan out there, you just must find it and release it to help people. This will allow you to stop complaining about you having no credit because you will be able to do business with a bank if you follow the above 3 steps. Another thing you should always have on your business checklist is: **"Keys to Success"**.

1.   Decide you want to do it (Plan)

2.   Take Action

3.   Keep changing approach if some part fails

Developing those skills in prison will allow you to stay out of prison and create opportunity. How will you be an asset to your community? With this answer, you will know if you' re ready to emerge from prison as a· success or failure. Your choice; your plan; your action; your success or failure; you have a choice. **OWNERSHIP IS KING!** Emerging from prison as your best self is key to your "Grand Plan". As you develop your business plan and idea for a business finance is key to any plan. There is a good website you should check out: **www.helpforfelons.org**. Because many felons and ex-offenders seek grants and loans this website was created to solve that problem. They have Loans and Grants for felons! The following is a short list of potential financing:

- Educational Pell Grants for felons

- Scholarships for felons

- Loans for felons

- Grant for felons

- Educational Loans for felons

- Private Loans for felons

- Small business loans for felons

- Payday Loans for felons

They also have the following information to help secure jobs, housing, etc.:

- Find Felony Friendly Housing

- Find Help Here

- ·Database for Felons

- Trucking Information Available

Information is there for you; just take the time to look into it and see if it can be useful to you, that's the purpose of this "Business Checklist", to provide you with information, so you can be successful in business and plan for the future. The

U.S. Small Business Administration (SBA} provides training and counseling for ex-offenders interested in opportunities to start their own business. To locate representatives offering free or low-cost training, in your area, the SBA hopes you visit **www.sba.gov/tools/local-assistance**. Another useful program the SBA has extended to ex-offenders that may be on parole or probation is the SBA's Microloan Intermediaries which provides small amounts of financial assistance to small business. Since 2015, the SBA rewrote the eligibility requirements allowing the microloan program to be extended to ex-offenders on parole or probation. To locateMicroloanIntermediarymyourareapleasevisit the website: **www.sba.gov/content/microloan-program**.

The SBA has another program designed to assist minority owned small businesses that were historically unable to win government contracts. The **8(A) Program** sets aside some procurements exclusively for competition among program participants. You must be certified by the SBA for admission in this program, to qualify, the company must be small, and majority owned and controlled by one or more socially and economically disadvantage U.S. Citizens. Net worth can't be greater than $250,000 (not including equity in home). Must have business for at least two years prior to applying; can be waived if potential for success is demonstrated. Visit www.sba.gov.

HUB ZONE CONTRACTING is another program offered to Underutilized Businesses in the HUB ZONE with high unemployment. Must apply for HUB ZONE Certification, SBA must approve your admission. To qualify, you must be located in HUB ZONE, it must be small under its NAICS code, it must be majority owned and controlled by "persons" who are U.S. Citizens, and 35% percent of its employees must live in a HUB ZONE. This program allows for minority owned business in poverty-stricken neighborhoods to get contracts from the federal government that it would otherwise never see. Visit sba.gov for more information and an application form.

Conclusion: Urban Revitalization

Prose Prisoners, we have come to a point where the rubber must meet the road and action must be put into your plans. I started off this book with knowledge/history about being poor, hungry, and driven to success. An education on the history of how our thriving communities turned into ghettos filled with crime and mayhem. Out of that despair emerged a people with strength and determination to rise out of those planned conditions of urban and rural America. Those hard times were where your Ph.D. was developed, proven, and used. Now, I want to show you the future just as I showed you the past or the "HOW" it happens. The solution is "Urban Revitalization" our planned investment in our own community using the methods of ownership in this book.

We as people of poverty always strived to build up our community. We need to get back to this concept look at people like Edward P. McCabe an African American man from Troy, New York, who went South in 1889 to Oklahoma to build communities and build he did. He wasn't alone, and around 1890-1900 many would spring up in Oklahoma, to help his people during Reconstruction, he took ads out for people to come to Oklahoma. Langston, Oklahoma (he named the land Langston, about 25 miles from Perry, Oklahoma). Around 1892, Langston was thriving with 25 businesses, a doctor's office, and a school. Telephones were installed around 1895 and in 1897, a black college was established. Back then people that had little means and lived in improvised towns, where they were subject to oppression and slavery, came together, pooled resources and built-up communities, the likes of which hasn't been repeated by their kids, grandkids, or cousins of this generation. Why? Coming out of slavery, they were subject to harsher treatment and laws than we face today. So, why? McCabe, a man who fought so hard to save his community that he sold his house to create a war chest to fight the racist laws that destroyed his dreams.

(Mainly the 7-1 decision by the Supreme Court in Plessy V. Ferguson (1896).) One of the worst decisions in the history of this country. "Separate but equal"-it confirmed the right to pass racist laws. Still, we fought and built our communities up with the things important to sustain life. Look at our communities now, we sell drugs on comers, kill for blocks, and when you boil it all down, we own nothing! Our grandfathers and grandmothers built not just blocks but thriving communities out of nothing, while being under pressure. Before the term: "Urban revitalization" was coined, they built and revitalized their own communities.

So, you get the picture clearly, let's talk about another powerful leader, who went beyond building communities, and built a 1,200-seat arena in Memphis.

Robert Reed church was his name, and he was wealthy, this was in (1889)! He was so wealthy that he bailed out the city of Memphis from bankruptcy. He built the park without loans or partners. Soon after he became a delegate at the Republican National Convention. All this from a formerly enslaved boy from Mississippi. He was a millionaire and the richest black man in the country. He helped Booker T. Washington, with the National Negro Business League, a black business network and think tank. Church interest was in black entrepreneurship and donated to black schools. Before Martin Luther King, Jr. and the other civil rights leaders dinned at the White House, Church and Washington were there with Roosevelt in the 1900s. He even got President Roosevelt to speak in Memphis at the Church Auditorium. (A quick note Robert Church the richest black man in America in 1880's-1900' s, share the first name with the richest black man in America today Robert Smith- history repeating itself). He also saw that his community didn't have a bank, so he opened a bank named Solvent Savings Bank & Trust Co., with this he became the first black owner of a bank in Memphis. Now he could lend a 3% percent and legally finance black business that wasn't getting loans from white banks, that wouldn't lend to black people. Did all this while saving churches that was foreclosed on by white banks. At the time of his death in August of 1912, he left his wife and 5 children and estate worth millions in 1912, a lot more in today' s money.

How many more leaders do you need to before you see that we need to get back to urban and rural "Revitalization", to bring our communities out of poverty? These Americans didn't wait to be rescued or taken care of by the Government they saw the lack of essential things a community needs to grow and built it, created opportunity for their community. Black-Wall Street wasn't a rap label as the rapper Game portrays it to be, it was thriving communities that had many black wealthy people who owned banks, Doctor Offices, Law firms, Stores, and businesses. Think of Alonzo Herndon, the owner of the country's largest black insurance company, "Atlanta Life Insurance", this was around 1906. Fourteen (14) years later he became Atlanta's first black millionaire.

Tulsa, Oklahoma existed, this is no myth. Oil was found there, and land owned by Creek Indians, African Americans flocked there for high paying oil jobs, but soon realized blacks couldn't work in the oil fields, essentially banned from oil riches. So those that left the south adopted and took jobs in the city at shops and stores. As always, the magician tricked us into believing we could gain in the richest of the oil boom, only to pass local laws that banned us from it. But one man saw that ban as an opportunity, his name was Ottowa W. Gurley, who moved to Tulsa and purchased 40 acres of land and built a grocery store on a dirt road. With the partnership of John, the Baptist Stratford, they developed an all-black district in Tulsa. Together they built housing, retail lots, alleys, and streets to accommodate the growing numbers of blacks flocking to Tulsa. Named a street Greenwood Ave and built a school and an African Methodist Church on Greenwood. They didn't stop there; they built Apartment buildings, homes, and the Gurley Hotel. These were builders of communities that created opportunity for their people who were living in poverty. A masonic lodge was built as was an employment agency. Where are these things in our community now? The history books are written by the winners, the suppression of these historical facts was done on purpose, you will never find this information in schools in our neighborhoods, and not even National black leaders could tell you this. I asked myself why? Why, are our community's hell holes? Were they always this improvised? Did we ever obtain wealth? Through these questions I did deep research to find out that we come from wealthy ancestors who built communities from nothing but dirt roads.

We had newspapers that delivered the news to us direct, papers like the Tulsa star whose publisher was an African American named A. J. Smitherman.

Remember, it just wasn't Tulsa, this was happening in urban black communities all over. Alonzo Herndon in Atlanta founded Sweet Auburn District, where professors and black elites called home. Memphis, Jacksonville, St. Louis, and Chicago. The promise of prosperity will always bring people into dying urban cities, but urban revitalization needs to happen first. That growth in the 21st Century needs to happen, to stop drugs, death, and high unemployment with low- wage jobs. All this growth didn't come from just men, but women also; the likes of Annie Malone in St. Louis; Madame C. J. Walker who at first sold hair products for Malone, moved away, and took Malone hair secrets to create her own hair product empire. Annie Malone didn't patent her Poro beauty products.

In the creation of these ghettos, we never had the knowledge about these before us, which thrived to build wealth on a scale that has yet to be duplicated in the 21st Century. Black wealth is overlooked by blacks and others and our economic gains have been washed from history. Schools teach slavery and civil rights, but not economic titans like the first black millionaire in America

"William Alexander Leidesdorff, John Drew, a stock trader who used a white broker to trade for him because at that time blacks couldn't trade; he also was the first black to own a bus line. To Mary Ellen Pleasant, who became wealthy trading commodities and was the proprietress of high-end boarding houses: another woman was Hannah Elias who helped build Harlem into a thriving city. Jeremiah Hamilton was the richest black man in New York and dubbed "The Prince of Darkness", he was a successful investor. That name came from being a ruthless Wall Street broker. We come from success, and we need to get back to that mind-set, we need to do as our ancestors did, one community at a time across the entire U.S.A. This is your look behind the curtain of black wealth and economic growth through revitalizing communities and building wealth. Your Ph.D. was birthed by these titans of economic success. You never knew these people existed; they are part of your drive, hunger, and your poor condition. The blueprint they laid their lives and fortunes on the line for needs to be picked back-up in our urban revitalization plans. If we neglect the past, we will never build an economic future with inclusion of urban and rural American's growth upward. Inequalities can nonstop us from achieving economic parity with other successful classes or groups in this country.

Poor and uneducated we are sent to prison, and we as people must wake- up and except the short comings of the generation before mine. They fought for Civil Right; we will fight for Economic and Financial Freedom for urban and rural America. Now we know the history of a planned assault on the poor and the history of success despite the chains of slavery. As a prisoner we play a role because we are the killers, drug dealers and pimps, who are destroying our communities instead of building them up and owning something. If we change our mind-set, the ghettos will become thriving urban and rural towns, cities, and counties. Urban Revitalization must start with the ones that are destroying it. Not to say the magician didn't do his part by placing drugs, redlining, disinvestment, and factoring jobs moving overseas in the late 60's and early 70's. But now we must recognize that we must do our part to fix this problem and our only chance is URBAN REVITALIZATION.

Create opportunity by building up the community and putting services and industry back in the ghettos. Banks, health grocery stores, farms, real estate, affordable housing (not Section 8), insurance agencies, doctors, medical facilities, rec. centers with STE programs, schools with 21st Century job training, etc. Pick your business and help your community, don't destroy what your ancestors tried to preserve for you. My next book or follow up to this book will be called: Prose Prisoner: Alternative Investments (Guide to Wealth), there I will show you how the 1% has built wealth and how you can build wealth playing by the rules of the rich. This book will not really be liked by the (rich) because I'm giving their secrets away to prisoners, who should use it to build empires and wealth for improvised neighborhoods.

How do we start our urban revitalization plan? Around 1925-1935, land ownership struck many people. The jobs that we are getting are not enough to gain home ownership, even in our poor ghettos, where housing values are extremely low. Laws have changed, mainly thanks to two black men who dared to buy 2 banks in Texas in the 1960s, by using a white man as the face of those banks. Their names were Bernard Garnett and Joe Morris. Garnett as a kid shined their shoes, he would listen to them discuss business, and potential investments. So, as he shined, he learned the rich way of doing business, remember this was in 1939 in Willis, Texas, where racism was part of the daily routine. The same bank he would shine shoes as a kid in front of, he would later own the bank and all the rich and middle-class money in the bank. (THINK ABOUT THAT!) At the peak of their rise, Garnett and Morris owned 177 properties around Texas and California. Garnett began giving loans to black businesses and people to buy houses. Soon after the feds raided their banks and licked them up for violating a loophole in the banking laws that said they didn't have to reveal who they were. Washington held hearings and Garnett stood-up to the racist system and talked about why two black men loaning money to black people from their own banks was a problem to the racist in Texas. Both Garnett and Morris were sentenced to 3 years in federal prison. Denied at every corner, Garnett created opportunity, used his financial knowledge he learned while shining shoes of Bank Executives, to buy 2 banks and 177 real estate holdings in California and Texas. Denied loans he brought banks, denied real estate investments, he marched on to put his life savings on the line .to prove he could find undervalued real estate in white communities. Because of his testimony in Washington, D.C. the Government in 1968 passed the Fair Housing Act that had clauses that said there can be no discrimination in housing based on race, gender, or religion.

Right now, Fannie Mae has set new rules for lending to black Americans. Now lenders must consider nontraditional credit data, which includes rent payments and utility bills payment history of a household of the applicant. Real Estate ownership is the first pillar of building wealth and is also considered passive income, which is the least taxed area of the business world. Another program allows low-down-payment options. The Community Development Block Grant Program is a U.S. Housing and Urban Development Program. Applicants can use the program funds down payment assistance up to 50% of the down payment required by the lender. Also, up to $500 is available for closing costs. In the 20th Century, the FTTA held blacks and rural Americans back from owning homes in certain areas, now they have loosened restrictions. Take advantage of all these programs, the first pillar is: HOME OWNERSHIP.

This ownership also includes stores, banks, rec. centers, schools, healthy grocery stores, hair salons, barbershops, stem buildings, and investment producing real estate. Wealth is generated from Assets, not liabilities! A pillar is just part of a broader agenda, we must formulate a agenda and the first is: Urban Revitalization and Rural Revitalization, formed around a common agenda that leads to people getting out of poverty but not moving out of the neighborhoods, but staying and building it up to a thriving asset building machine, where ownership is the central focus. Why do we always say what the problem is, but don't have a plan to accomplish this? The magician doesn't lend or loan money to my business; so, what! Buy or start your own bank and pool community resources to lend or loan to your own poverty-stricken neighborhoods. Our market value is 1.2 trillion dollars! But it's not concentrated in improvised ghettos; we spend it outside our communities where we perceive that these people have your best interest. Lol! Spend in your community loan moan money in your community, own businesses in your community, and these improvised ghettos will be thriving middle and upper-class neighborhoods. Our sword to wield is our 1.2 trillion Dollar spending a year around this country. Our culture is so much about being famous and wearing the latest foreign designers, when there are successful people in your community designing on the same level as Gucci. Stop trying to be famous or LG. and build an empire. We need to move beyond poverty and focusing on Urban Revitalization is the key to fixing poverty.

Another pillar is EDUCATION, not K-12 school type of education, but teaching our kids 21st Century things that will help them obtain financial freedom. Stem schools, financial literacy, how to balance a check book, how to build credit, obtain loans, start companies, own their own businesses, and how to become entrepreneurs. Teaching this to kids in abject poverty will dismantle the magician's power over the brain, K-12 is a trap and a business gone out of control. Either we develop a reclamation plan for these schools in these ghettos or continue to fail our kids of the future. Education about basic life things is good, but for poor kids we need small business teachings not AP level mathematics, they won't use in daily life. Learn to balance a check book; learn how to file taxes and read the tax code will be more effective for kids in abject poverty than learning eight hours of useless information that won't even lift their standard test scores. Based on a zip code you can tell kids success rates, which is sad. Lack of resources, poverty, also causes problems for success in these communities. This also leads to uneducated kids being pushed to prisons at alarming rates. Fix the education problem; retool 21st Century teaching and you will overnight rebuild urban and rural America. Can't get in M.I.T.? Build our own M.I.T. in these poverty-stricken ghettos. Reading and math scores in Baltimore, where I'm from, are less than 20 percent. Teachers and school CEO's have failed these kids while your tax dollars are wasted every year in this prison pipe-line schools. Prepare these kids for building businesses and not working for rich people after college while paying them back for loans you got to go to college. Education can only be an equalizer if it's the right education. Some students excel in K-12 in these ghettos, but that's less than one percent of the students. We don't need robots, or 9 to 5 zombies, to stop abject poverty we need CEOs of business, entrepreneur to teach financial literacy, real estate investors and 21st Century urban and rural revitalization efforts to come back to our poverty-stricken ghettos we have left behind. I plan to do just that, one ghetto at a time.

My mind set allows me to see clearly, think without limits and see opportunity where others see trash. These two pillars: Home Ownership and 21st Century Education is the starting point to a total urban and rural revitalization plan. Not owning a home and living in it but buy a home as an "asset" and create an income producing property. Living in a house you own is not going to get you out of financial trouble from living paycheck to paycheck. Use debt and taxes, as the rich do to become financially independent. In my next book Prose Prisoner: Alternative Investments (Guide to Wealth). I will show you how to build true wealth by first teaching you financial education. Then show you how to acquire assets using debt and in some cases, legally show you how to not pay taxes on earned income and real estate.

With this book and the next book, you will have your Financial Education and Grand Plan to rebuild and become wealthy as a prisoner. Urban revitalization will help your community uplift out of poverty, stop waiting for the government and other people to help you. Change starts with you; you see something wrong; change it. I will close how I started, with critical thoughts. My goal has been to give you the history, so you can change the future, also I have been guiding you out of poverty and into financial freedom, and lastly I have showed you that your condition of poverty and plight was planned, but what the magician didn't expect was that we didn't need to go to school for a Ph.D. because we already had one, just by growing up Poor, Hungry and Driven to Success.

About the Author

Prison takes away everything in its destructive path to destroy the human spirit. It is like a storm that pours so much rain and has such powerful winds that it destroys everything in its path.

My name is C. A. Knuckles. Like you, I'm incarcerated. I've been in a Maryland prison since the tender age of 15. To date, I've served 15 years here.

My growth hasn't come easy, as a child starting out in an adult prison. I'm serving time for Second Degree Attempted Murder, and prison was a crash course I really wasn't ready for. At an early age, as a teenager, I was a gang member. But prison wasn't the place to mess up and get stuck. I almost lost all chance of freedom because that gang really didn't care whether I lived or died in prison.

So, at 17 years old I got out, took the consequences, and moved on to better my life. To this day, it is the best decision I've ever made. Never was I dumb; I have what you call a dangerous combination: street smarts and book smarts. An "A" student in school, my yearning for knowledge put me on the path of business success. That's what led me to write this book, a "how-to guide" for likeminded prisoners who might have thought they could never possibly invest in these fields.

There might have even been fellow prisoners saying, "You can't do that," or even family members. Now here is your chance and guide to do what they think is impossible. Remember, you're bigger than your situation.

We have been "mind fucked" into thinking selling drugs is the only way to meet our financial goals. We are led to think that drug dealers are role models, with money and cars. I'm a numbers guy. Statistics are great forecasters. So, add up how many drug dealers you know, then look at the number of them who made it off the streets successfully without going to prison, snitching to stay out of prison, or dying before their time. That's not success, that's insane.

We have done the same thing repeatedly for the past 40-50 years, to no avail. Albert Einstein said: "Insanity is doing the same thing over and over and expecting a different outcome." Look in the mirror. It is time to take a chance on something other than losing. The first step is already done – you have either brought this book or somebody let you borrow it. Success stories are the guys who changed their thinking. You must first gain knowledge and then execute your plan like I did. Then you can become financially independent, and not fall victim to Einstein's definition of insanity.

FREEBIRD PUBLISHERS

Thanks for your interest in Freebird Publishers!

We value our customers and would love to hear from you! Reviews are an important part in bringing you quality publications. We love hearing from our readers-rather it's good or bad (though we strive for the best)!

If you could take the time to review/rate any publication you've purchased with Freebird Publishers we would appreciate it!

If your loved one uses Amazon, have them post your review on the books you've read. This will help us tremendously, in providing future publications that are even more useful to our readers and growing our business.

Amazon works off of a 5 star rating system. When having your loved one rate us be sure to give them your chosen star number as well as a written review. Though written reviews aren't required, we truly appreciate hearing from you.

CURRENT FULL COLOR CATALOG

92-Pages filled with books, gifts and services for prisoners

We have created four different versions of our new catalog A: Complete B:No Pen Pal Content C:No Sexy Photo Content D:No Pen Pal and Sexy Content. Available in full Color or B&W (please specify) please make sure you order the correct catalog based on your prison mail room regulations. We are not responsible for rejected or lost in the mail catalogs. Send SASE for info on stamp options.

Freebird Publishers Book Selection Includes:

- Ask. Believe. Receive.: Our Power to Create Our Own Destiny
- Celebrity Female Star Power
- Cell Chef 1 & 2
- Cellpreneur: The Millionaire Prisoner's Guidebook
- Chapter 7 Bankruptcy: Seven Steps to Financial Freedom
- Convicted Creations Cookbook
- Cooking With Hot Water
- DIY for Prisoners
- Federal Rules of Criminal Procedures Pocket Guide
- Federal Rules of Evidence Pocket Guide
- Fine Dining Cookbook 1, 2, 3
- Freebird Publisher's Gift Look Book
- Get Money: Self Educate, Get Rich, & Enjoy Life (3 book series)
- Habeas Corpus Manual
- Hobo Pete and the Ghost Train
- Hot Girl Safari: Non-Nude Photo Book
- How to Write a Good Letter From Prison
- Ineffective Assistance of Counsel
- Inmate Shopper
- Inmate Shopper Censored
- Introduction to Financial Success
- Kitty Kat: Adult Entertainment Resource Book
- Life With a Record
- Locked Down Cookin'
- Locked Up Love Letters: Becoming the Perfect Pen Pal
- Parent to Parent: Raising Children from Prison
- Penacon Presents: The Prisoners Guide to Being a Perfect Pen Pal
- Pen Pal Success: The Ultimate Guide to Getting & Keeping Pen Pals
- Pen Pals: A Personal Guide for Prisoners
- Pillow Talk: Adult Non-Nude Photo Book
- Post-Conviction Relief Series (Books 1-7)
- Prison Health Handbook
- Prison Legal Guide
- Prison Picasso
- Prisoner's Communication Guidelines for Navigating in Prison
- Prisonyland Adult Coloring Book
- Pro Se Guide to Legal Research & Writing
- Pro Se Prisoner: How to Buy Stocks and Bitcoin
- Pro Se Section 1983 Manual
- Section 2254 Pro Se Guide to Winning Federal Relief
- Soft Shots: Adult Non-Nude Photo Book
- The Best 500 Non-Profit Organizations for Prisoners & Their Families
- Weight Loss Unlocked
- Write & Get Paid

CATALOG ONLY $5 - SHIPS BY FIRST CLASS MAIL
ADDITIONAL OPTION: add $5 for Shipping and Handling with Tracking

PayPal

NO ORDER FORM NEEDED CLEARLY WRITE ON PAPER & SEND PAYMENT TO:
FREEBIRD PUBLISHERS 221 Pearl St., Ste. 541, North Dighton, MA 02764
www.FreebirdPublishers.com Diane@FreebirdPublishers.com Text/Phone: 774-406-8682
We accept all forms of payment. Plus Venmo & CashApp! Venmo: @FreebirdPublishers CashApp: $FreebirdPublishers

Made in the USA
Coppell, TX
04 December 2024

41757887R00105